ALSO BY FRANCINE RUSSO

They're Your Parents, Too!: How Siblings Can Survive Their
Parents' Aging Without Driving Each Other Crazy

Love
After 50

How to Find It, Enjoy It, and Keep It

FRANCINE RUSSO

Simon & Schuster

New York   London   Toronto   Sydney   New Delhi

Simon & Schuster
1230 Avenue of the Americas
New York, NY 10020

First Simon & Schuster hardcover edition July 2021

SIMON & SCHUSTER and colophon are registered trademarks of Simon & Schuster, Inc.

For information about special discounts for bulk purchases, please contact
Simon & Schuster Special Sales at 1-866-506-1949 or business@simonandschuster.com.

The Simon & Schuster Speakers Bureau can bring authors to your live event.
For more information or to book an event, contact the Simon & Schuster Speakers Bureau
at 1-866-248-3049 or visit our website at www.simonspeakers.com.

Interior design by Ruth Lee-Mui

Manufactured in the United States of America

1   3   5   7   9   10   8   6   4   2

Library of Congress Cataloging-in-Publication Data
Names: Russo, Francine, author.
Title: Love after 50 : how to find it, enjoy it, and keep it / Francine
Russo.
Other titles: Love after fifty
Description: New York : Simon & Schuster, [2021] | Includes bibliographical
references. | Summary: "This ultimate, comprehensive, and intimate guide
will help you find and keep love after 50"—Provided by publisher.
Identifiers: LCCN 2020043556 | ISBN 9781982108540 (hardcover) | ISBN
9781982108564 (ebook)
Subjects: LCSH: Man-woman relationships. | Interpersonal attraction. |
Middle-aged persons.
Classification: LCC HQ801 .R926 2021 | DDC 306.7—dc23
LC record available at https://lccn.loc.gov/2020043556

ISBN 978-1-9821-0854-0
ISBN 978-1-9821-0856-4 (ebook)

To Michael and my children:
Sara, Joanna, Justin, Lindsey, and Brennan

And to the memory of Edward Churnside

Contents

Preface

Timing has shaped every aspect of my life. Why did I become a writer? Because there were too many PhDs in English: Good luck finding a teaching job. After a few false starts, I plunged into journalism as a freelancer. Freelancers live on their story ideas. I got them by noticing new trends among people I knew. The first one I wrote about became a classic cover story for *New York* magazine: "Live-in Divorce: Tortured Couples Who Have to Live Together."

Many years later, I saw folks around me coping with a new life passage: the aging of parents who needed long-term care; they were living longer than ever before. I saw this passage in my own life and that of others. My observations and research became my first book: *They're Your Parents, Too!: How Siblings Can Survive Their Parents' Aging Without Driving Each Other Crazy.*

Lately, I've noticed a way more upbeat trend in the over-fifty crowd: a boom in new romances and relationships. Everybody I knew had stories to tell of never-married, widowed, or divorced friends or relatives falling in love. Whether they dated long-term or long-distance, moved in together, got married, or did some combination of the above, the subjects of these stories were amazingly, unexpectedly happy. Many said it was their best relationship ever!

Suddenly, researchers took note and scrambled to learn more about this unprecedented phenomenon of later-life partnering. They showed how our longer life spans, changing attitudes to marriage and divorce, and evolving cultural views fueled this tsunami of later-life love.

This was a story I knew from the inside. I'm lucky. I've had two wonderful marriages. The first, with Alan, was typical of young marriages. We were both ambitious. He was a lawyer climbing the ladder at a Wall Street firm that demanded countless hours. I loved him intensely; I was proud of him. But I was needy and struggling, especially after I lost my university teaching job. When we had our two girls, our family became our focus, and we had to fight for time as a couple. Sometimes we fought with each other. By our forties, we'd grown up some, fought less, and accepted ourselves and each other more. We'd found our footing in our careers. The girls were in school, and life was easier. Then, at the awful age of forty-nine, Alan was struck down by a heart attack and died. Our girls were nine and fifteen, and my world changed.

For several years, I was driven to keep us all as safe and stable as possible. I did date a bit and had some brief relationships. Then, when my younger daughter went off to college, I met Chris.

Chris and I had everything in common. We were widowed single parents, writers, and avid cyclists. Like me, he'd dropped out as an English professor and struggled to make a living. We married in our late fifties when our kids were almost grown, and we were less career-ladder-focused. Our love was deeply satisfying, suffused with gratitude that we'd found each other. Although he died too soon—after four years of marriage—of lung cancer, I never regretted for an instant that I'd loved him, despite my devastating grief. I did wonder, though, whether I could risk love again.

I could. I did. I'm someone who thrives in an intimate partnership. Four years after Chris died, I felt ready. I'd already learned how to date online (I met Chris that way). I knew the kind of partner I wanted, and in my late sixties, I surprised myself. I was open to meeting men I never would have considered in the past. Money or lack of it didn't matter. I'd moved to an apartment I could afford on my own. Status and ambition were irrelevant. Kids or no kids? Whatever.

Both with Chris and now with Michael, my partner of five years, I have become part of this wave of later-life partnering. Whether they meet online or another way, the numbers of divorced people who remarry (67 percent of 55-to-64-year-olds, and 50 percent of those 65 and older) partially reveal the scope of this mega-trend. Add in couples who cohabitate or form intimate partnerships without sharing a home, and you begin to see how huge the trend is. It's happening because we are the first to live so long in such good health and to divorce in such great numbers after age fifty. Although less common among folks in their fifties and sixties, the widowed are also repartnering.

Research shows that, as a group, we're experiencing a kind of union that's not only different from but often *better* than any before, even if we were happily married. Whether you're fifty or seventy, your age fosters a unique potential for love. As partners, you're probably more emotionally stable, more focused on the present and your relationship than earlier. Your children are probably not the center of your everyday life. If you work, you're probably less career-driven. The drive to achieve, studies show, tends to decline with age.

Emotional growth, however, presents an almost limitless prospect. In her study of couples in later-life second marriages, Israeli psychologist Chaya Koren found that both men and women expressed an increased sense of him- or herself as an individual in the new marriage. Koren describes this as the sense of "greater 'I-ness' (separateness)" in the new marriage rather than the dominant feeling of "total 'we-ness' (togetherness)" in the earlier marriage. For women, in particular, this comes from an increased ability to negotiate power, money, and roles.

Both men and women in Koren's study felt their new marriage was *different* from their first: either better or not comparable. Other researchers have found that later-life relationships offer greater opportunity for psychological growth and emotional differentiation, having a secure sense of selfhood and the emotional boundaries between themselves and others. This greater selfhood, psychologists agree, enables greater intimacy.

I've been so fulfilled in my later-life loves. I've learned how to meet the emotional and practical challenges of love at our stage of life:

- finding the right partner
- making the relationship work
- creating a satisfying sexual life
- dealing with two established households
- accommodating differences in income and taste
- One *big* issue is adult children. Oh, boy, can they present problems (as well as joys) for a new couple. I hope *Love After 50* will help you maximize your remarkable opportunities for love. I will also help you navigate the occasionally difficult realities that go with creating this astonishing new love in the time of wisdom.

Section I

Prepare Yourself

Chapter One

Do the Headwork

O ver fifty? You're in luck. You've heard the stories or seen the couples all around you. People who seem far less likely than you have found love. *My fifty-five-year-old girlfriend just got married, and she hadn't had a date in ten years. My sixty-six-year-old aunt just moved in with a guy she's crazy about. My eighty-year-old uncle, who's been single forever, is madly in love!*

Now is your time to find the love you've always wanted. If you've had unfulfilling relationships so far, you're now poised to find a *deeply* satisfying one. If you were happily married, you may find an equally wonderful partnership, different but in some ways even better. For some, this will be easy. Others will have to work harder.

Even if this does not come easily to you, your age is an *advantage*. Look at the facts.

In study after study, Stanford's Laura Carstensen and her colleagues have shown that people your age are more emotionally stable than younger people. You focus more on the positive; you steer away from stress and conflict when you can; you invest your energies in the people and things that mean most to you. These changes set you up for a richly rewarding love. Carstensen reckons there's no better stage of life for finding it.

In addition, some life pressures have fallen away. You're almost certainly free of hands-on child rearing. If you're working, you're probably less career-ladder-focused than before. One sixty-four-year-old divorced executive says that until she retired, work and family (an aging mother and a teenage daughter) were her priorities. She'd dated but remained emotionally aloof. She says, "The wonderful relationship I'm in now could not have existed even five years ago."

Even if you do have baggage, as Kansas City therapist and marriage counselor Mark McGonigle told me, "By now, most folks have mapped out their own psychological terrain. In therapy, they tend to be reflective people trying to learn from their experience. The first half of life is about accumulating. The second half is about getting rid of what you don't need."

I can't stress this enough. Now more than ever before, you are primed for a relationship in which you have a greater sense of self and an expanded capacity for intimacy.

Getting to this place was harder for me than you might think, given that I'd been in a reasonably good marriage for twenty-two years. Alan and I had married young. He was anxious and neurotic. So was I, as well as desperately needy. We loved each other. We needed each other. We fought about things big and ridiculously small. We had power struggles. We indulged ourselves. In many ways, we were and remained big babies, even after our two daughters were born and grew up, healthy and strong, with some of their parents' imperfections inevitably part of them.

The moment I really began to grow up was the night Alan had a heart attack and died in the hospital. It was six the next morning when I crept into our girls' room and told them they weren't going to school that day: "Daddy died last night."

On that October night in 1993, I was transformed from a wife to a widow and from a mother to a single parent. Parenting took on a passionate and acutely protective edge. I felt driven to shelter my girls from further pain and upheaval, to keep our lives as stable as possible. My responsibilities became heavier because I shouldered them alone. But I had more freedom, too. If I chose to try to make a go of full-time freelance magazine writing, it was my risk to take, and I could and would manage the consequences.

But being alone? Without someone to love me and hold me and comfort me? Without someone to share my life? That terrified me. I was forty-six. Would I be alone for the rest of my life? I needed reassurance that I would be with someone again. Six months after we laid Alan in his grave, while I was still reeling with grief, I started meeting people through the precursor to online dating: the personal ads in *New York* magazine. I never said a word about this to my girls. I wouldn't inflict that stress on them.

The first man I dated offered the romance and passion my stable marriage had lacked. He was right out of the *Girls' Romances* comic books I'd devoured at age thirteen. Well, maybe not that handsome. But he was wealthy and piloted a small airplane. On our second date, he parked his car along a deserted Hudson River pier, played Edith Piaf on the car radio, and danced with me! I was a total sucker for this treatment. I'd been craving it all my life. He told me I was amazing and smarter than any woman he'd ever been with. He desired me. He wrote me poems. It was heaven, at least for a couple of months.

We went to bed. Afterward I cried. Letting someone take Alan's role made my beloved husband feel both painfully present and more out of reach than ever before. My grief was redoubled. By the third month with this new man, I started recognizing him for the controlling guy he was. He'd told me from the start that he'd been in a long-term relationship and was in the process of disentangling himself from it. I soon learned that she'd been his mistress while he was married and after. He supported her and expected her to be totally available for him. He'd installed a phone in her apartment that no one else could use. By our fifth month together, I realized he was still seeing her. I broke it off. It was painful to have that space emptied out again so abruptly.

I was thrown back into my searing grief for Alan, the grief I'd been trying to outrun by having this relationship. It was far too soon for a serious relationship; I couldn't escape the mourning I still had to do. Yet I learned from that little romance. I found out I was still a desirable woman and was unlikely to spend my life alone.

Even more, I realized I had to get stronger. Now. No matter how many girlfriends I called when I felt desperately alone, I couldn't escape my pain. It was like a fire: I had to walk through it to get to the other side. At times it felt excruciating and never-ending. But it did ebb and flow. And eventually, the fits of intense grief struck less regularly. I grew stronger because I had no other option.

I was in therapy now. I discovered the difference between grief and depression, which I sometimes fell into. Those were times when I felt hopeless and clung to my grief rather than looking ahead. I was also learning about dating, about the kind of men I chose to meet and those I dismissed. Over the ten years between my marriages, I'm sure I met more than a hundred men. I had several relationships lasting a year or more. I made mistakes, lots and lots of them. Mostly, I learned from them.

I did a lot of the headwork I talk about in this chapter and throughout this book; that gave me the emotional growth I needed to eventually choose Chris as my second husband. We shared so much:

being widowed, being single parents, being writers who'd once been college literature teachers. We loved to cycle. We confessed our foibles of dating foolishly and staying too long in relationships that were wrong for us. We were so damned grateful to have found each other.

We had love and passion and romance, too. (At the beginning, he wrote me a love note every day.) We had true intimacy. We'd both figured out what we'd done wrong or wished we'd done right in our marriages. We were the beneficiaries of each other's wisdom, and this was also a function of our age. We were fifty-five when we married.

You have your own story. Parts of it are like mine. Parts of it are like those of the scores of women and men who shared their experiences for this book: single, divorced, and widowed. We have all suffered pain and loss and heartbreak. We've learned from these experiences, growing emotionally, eventually finding amazing later-life love.

You may already have done this psychological work or at least some of it. You may still have much to do. You'll be surprised at how much you can still learn.

Are you ready? Before you embark on your search for a mate, think about these questions. Be as honest as you can, even if it hurts.

Do You Need to Do Some Headwork First?

Ask Yourself

- Do I fully understand who I am and what I need *now*?
- Am I available to new people in my life, or do I put up barriers?
- Am I desperate for a partner?
- Do I feel strong enough to take risks?

- Do I believe no one could make me as happy as my ex or my late spouse did?
- Do I feel unlovable?
- Do I need to clear space and time in my life to devote to an intimate relationship?
- Do the relationships I've had fall short of what I want?
- Have I let go of my anger? Or am I still, internally, arguing with that #*&&xx*!!!?

If any of these questions spark feelings or thoughts within you, you'll find greater success in love if you work on yourself before and during this journey. I hope as you read these stories from real people and the insights I share from experts, you'll reflect on how they apply to you. Some people find therapy helpful. I certainly did. Whatever tools you use, you are the one who has to do the work. Stay open, be strong, and be patient: You will get there.

New York psychotherapist Stephanie Manes advises older people seeking a great relationship: "Take the time to do the psychological work, to know yourself well enough to be responsible for yourself. If you do, you'll know when your reactions to someone are *your stuff*, and that way, you don't look across the table and say (or think), 'Why are you making me feel this way?'"

Get Yourself in the Best Emotional and Physical Shape You Can

Dating when you feel miserable or desperate is unlikely to attract the love you so badly want.

This was advice I heard often during the years after Alan's death. It was advice I just didn't get. When I wasn't in a relationship, I was *lonely*. How could I not be? My children couldn't give me the adult companionship I craved. My best friends were married or in relationships. I tried to make new friends, but it was hard. I developed friendships with a couple of women who were single and also interested in dating. That helped, but I still missed having a lover and companion.

I worked on enjoying time on my own. First I tried traveling. I did it sometimes alone, sometimes with a group. While visiting Amsterdam, I rediscovered my childhood love of cycling. When I came home, I bought a bike and became an avid cyclist. I joined bike clubs and did day trips with groups. I commuted to work by bike every day, even in the rain, wearing a waterproof poncho. On my bike, I didn't need anyone else. Pedaling along the river with the wind in my hair, I felt energized and happy. When sad thoughts entered my head, I let myself cry while in motion and the sadness passed. On otherwise lonely Saturday nights, I'd go to a theater and afterward, watch the crowd of people passing by outside a café. There were babies and dogs and fun exchanges with couples, old and young. I sometimes felt lonely but I also felt good that I could take care of myself and fill my own needs.

I threw myself into my writing work as well. I wrote more articles for more magazines, and I found the work sustaining.

All my life I'd felt an emptiness inside. I expected Alan to fill it and that's one reason we fought. Although I still very much wanted a partner, I felt better about myself now that I didn't feel desperate.

It's human to want to connect intimately with another person. Don't give yourself a hard time if you really want this. Desperation, however, is counterproductive to finding a healthy relationship. You need to find a way to be "okay" enough on your own, despite not wanting to be alone. This is not easy, acknowledges Manes. "You have to keep two opposing ideas in your mind at once," she says. "On the one hand, you need to be open, optimistic and hopeful. On the other, you have to live with the idea that this might not happen. The way you do this is to fall in love with your own life."

Learning to be independent, to fill needs no one else can fill for you, is an essential step to creating a fulfilling intimate relationship. Everyone I spoke to who found lasting love spent time learning to do this. Experiment to find out what you enjoy. And don't try dating if you don't feel ready. First work on just feeling okay.

Care for Yourself with Kindness

- Get enough sleep. If you can't, get tips from the National Sleep Foundation.
- Eat regularly and nutritiously. If you're feeling overweight and don't like it, take control of your eating with a healthy weight-loss plan. (I've found that when everything else feels out of control, being able to control *something* empowers me.)
- Exercise. Do whatever you like, alone or with others: Walk, run, cycle, or take a salsa class. Exercise fights depression and rage.
- Shut off your phone and go outside. Look at a tree or a flower

or a cloud. Breathe the wind; feel the sun. Smile at a baby; pet a dog. Say good morning to a stranger.
- Get touched. Have a massage or a pedicure. Get hugs from family and friends.

Practice Gratitude

When you're feeling like life has destroyed you, try noticing those who have it worse. A woman who met people dancing found out that some were recovering from a catastrophe worse than a cheating husband. Practice being grateful for what you have: food and shelter, family and friends, work, a home, a skill, a body that works.

Do Something for Others

When you do something for others, research shows it's good for you, too. At a minimum, you stop thinking about your own misery for a while. Helping makes you feel valuable. It releases feel-good hormones like dopamine and oxytocin. You don't have to volunteer in a cancer ward. Just listen supportively to a friend who's upset. Stop your car and wave an anxious pedestrian across the street. Assist someone with a cane and a heavily laden shopping cart across the parking lot. Reassure the terrified new cashier that her mistake wasn't so terrible and she'll get better with experience.

Practice Mindfulness

Mindfulness is being in the moment, being aware of all our senses, what we're seeing, hearing, smelling, tasting, feeling. I get closest to this at breakfast. I set the table with my English china, my teapot kept warm in a rose-covered tea cozy and my delicate pitcher full of steamed milk. Then after the flurry of preparation, I take several long, deep breaths until my heart slows and I grow calm. I feel the warm tea slide over my tongue and down my throat. When I lift my antique silver spoon filled with berries and cereal to my mouth, I enjoy the color, the crunch, and the taste. I center a mouthful on my tongue and savor the burst of flavors. I gaze at the tree outside my window bending in the breeze off the river.

When I am in that moment, when *you* are in *your* moment, you're not rehashing your past or obsessing about your future. You're enjoying a *respite* from pain.

Mindfulness is a big subject; there are many ways to learn and use it. It can help you accept what is, rather than fighting it. It can help you notice recurrent negative or dysfunctional thoughts you'd like to banish. It can reduce depression, anger, and anxiety.

Many disciplines use mindfulness, such as yoga and meditation. Apps for your phone (Aura, Calm, and Insight Timer, for example) can help you practice mindfulness on your own.

Don't be discouraged if you find mindfulness difficult at first. Keep at it and you will enjoy its benefits.

Find What's Lovable about You — and Believe in It

If you've always doubted your value and lovability, now's the time to shore it up. If you're feeling unsure, remind yourself frequently of the many good things you can bring to a relationship.

- List the qualities you're proud of, for example: I'm well organized, a good parent, a hard worker, an empathic person. I show up for my friends. I have a sense of humor and make people laugh.
- Think back on all those who have cared about you: family, friends, colleagues.
- Ask your close friends what they find lovable about you. Believe what they say and put it on your list.
- This is not for everyone, but if you have a small supportive "friends" group on social media, you might say you're feeling a little down on yourself and it would help if they'd mention good traits they've noticed about you. "One of my clients did this," says therapist Jill Whitney. "She got such a flood of good stuff that it made her cry."
- Train yourself to notice negative thoughts about yourself. Replace those thoughts with the positive items on your list. If you do this over and over, you will sooner or later repel the destructive thoughts.

Christine* had been married ten years to a man who regularly called her "stupid." After she divorced him, she thought about who

---

*Names noted with an asterisk are pseudonyms to protect the privacy of my interviewees.

she wanted to be now. First she gave herself credit for the courage it took to end her marriage. She had two goals for her remade identity. "I had a teenage girl at home, and I wanted to go from a bad example to a good model for her of a strong woman," she says. "And I was strong. I just lacked confidence."

The second part of her new identity evolved as she tried to make sense of the investments that came with her divorce settlement. She realized that, far from being stupid, she had a real head for investing. She managed her own portfolio so well, in fact, that she qualified for a training program at a major investment firm. She's now a successful wealth manager.

Make Sure You're Healed from Your Divorce

Divorce can crush your spirit. Whether you initiated it or had it sprung on you, it can fill you with a sense of failure and loss. Your faith in yourself, your judgment, and your worth suffer. Grief is almost certain. Anger can rage for years. If you divorced recently, take the time you need to heal before you're ready for a new relationship.

Many people are shocked when their husband or wife asks for a divorce. This happens even if you struggled for years with entrenched issues and had couples therapy without solving anything. Maybe you soldiered on, each with your own dissatisfaction and unhappiness. Yet when she finally says the words "I want a divorce," you can't believe it. Maybe you were living in denial, knowing and yet not knowing that your marriage was dissolving. Or maybe you knew but hoped against hope that you could save it. Either way, there is a period of shock and, for some, numbness.

Mourn Your Loss

Sadness is inevitable when your marriage ends, even if you and your spouse were the rare amicable but mismatched couple who's agreed to separate once the kids were grown. This was true of Judith. The fifty-nine-year-old woman and her husband had recognized years before that apart from their shared love for their three children, they had absolutely nothing in common. They spent little time together and stopped having sex. You might imagine there was little to mourn. Yet five months after she moved into her own apartment, Judith was assailed by grief. She remembers sitting at dinner with a date and asking herself, *What happened to my life? Who is this person?* "I felt a disconnect," she says. "I was mourning leaving my house. I missed my old life. Even though it wasn't the life I wanted, I was attached to it."

After years of sharing a home and a life, many people feel sad coming home to an empty house, sleeping alone, having no one to chitchat with about their day or the idiot who sideswiped them on the way home. "You have to grieve not only for the loss of the person but also for the ideal of the marriage itself," says psychotherapist Krista Jarvis. "One of the most poignant losses is that of the imagined future you would have had with this person."

Before his wife told him that she wanted a divorce, Gary* had looked forward to a golden era together when the kids were adults. He foresaw how they would knit together as a couple again, be as they'd been before the children. They'd have sex again! He'd told himself that having the kids was why they hadn't had sex in a decade.

He grew nostalgic recalling their last Thanksgiving together with the kids, now in their twenties. "That was the point I'd been waiting for, when my kids were adults and we could talk to each other as adults," he recalls. "That's when my wife and I would rekindle our relationship . . . Little did I know."

Mourning takes time. You have to give it that time, whether it's six months, a year, or longer. Feeling sad hurts, but it's normal. You'll need to sit in that discomfort for as long as it takes. It won't be easy or painless. But you must *accept* your loss, stop fighting or rehashing it, and move on. That's the key to getting to a happier future.

There are many ways to find comfort as you mourn. Leaning on friends and family can help. Throwing yourself into responsibilities can sustain you.

As you move through the pain, says therapist Karen Osterle, keep in mind one positive thought: The end of a relationship brings an unexpected opportunity—a "forced rebirth," to use her words.

If you find yourself so mired in sadness that you can't move forward, you may well be depressed. How can you tell the difference? If you feel sad about your loss and you cry and it hurts, that's normal. If you continually feel hopeless about any possible future, you may be depressed. Start with talk therapy and go from there, suggests Osterle. You may need antidepressants. If so, your therapist can guide you to a good medical expert who can determine what medication could help.

Do You Feel Shame or Guilt About Your Divorce?

Maybe you were the one who got cheated on. Maybe you were the one left with a financial mess when your ex took off. Was it you who suffered years of abuse? So why do *you* feel shame? What are *you* guilty of?

It makes no sense to other people, but many divorced people feel ashamed. Bonnie, for example, a fifty-year-old with three young children, was flooded with shame when her husband told her he'd been unfaithful and wanted to leave. She tried to save their marriage, but he was ready to go: He'd secretly separated his assets, leaving her with big money troubles. She had no choice but to file for divorce.

"I was afraid to tell anyone," she says. "I always put us up as a happy family. I felt I had failed to be a good enough wife."

In fact, telling—talking to people you trust—is the best antidote to shame.

How to Counteract Shame and Self-Blame with Reality

When you're blaming yourself for your divorce, pretend you're not yourself. Right now, imagine that a good friend, let's call her Eileen, has poured out the exact same story as yours. Imagine these are *her* feelings and thoughts, not yours. Write out your feelings, and then write what you think you would tell her.

- *I feel terribly ashamed.* Seriously? Oh, honey, why should *you* feel ashamed? He was the one who cheated. He was the one who racked up debts and didn't pay the mortgage. He was the one who criticized you and called you names when you were working really hard to make him happy. If anyone should be ashamed, he's the one!
- *There must be something seriously wrong with me or my marriage wouldn't have broken up.* If that's true, then everyone who gets divorced has something seriously wrong with them. Marriages break up for lots of reasons. People grow apart. The stress of kids and work and money wears them down

so they don't communicate well. People's needs change, and what was a good marriage at twenty-five might not work so well in your forties or fifties. Life happens. Give yourself a break.

- *If I were more attractive, my husband would have been faithful.* That's ridiculous. You're plenty attractive. Don't let anyone tell you that, especially the voice in your head.

- *I must have been an idiot not to see the clues.* Why would you think he was unfaithful? You trusted him. You grew up in a family where nobody cheated. It just wasn't in your vocabulary. So many husbands and wives have a blind spot where they can't see evidence of cheating even when outsiders might. It's a truism. *The spouse is always the last to know.* When you love someone so much, you believe him. You're just human, not an idiot.

- *I have no backbone or I wouldn't have tolerated being treated like that.* Okay, maybe you should've stood up for yourself more. But you've learned that lesson. Your next relationship will be better. And stop shaking your head. You *will* have another relationship, and I'm convinced what you're learning now will make it a happier one.

Your feelings are different from those of this hypothetical person, of course, but your conclusions may be just as flawed. Before or after you write down your feelings, tell them to a couple of good friends. Write on your list what *they* say. Then READ it regularly to ward off these destructive thoughts and counteract them when they occur.

Give yourself time to work through your self-blaming and start to evaluate your responsibility more realistically.

"Shame is how we think others evaluate us," explains Washington University psychology professor Brian Carpenter. "A person may think they're bad, but that's not always reality."

Once Bonnie began sharing her story with friends, they rallied to support her. Some told her they'd noticed things about her husband that worried them. They'd never believed that her marriage was perfect.

Bonnie had been blaming herself for everything. Over and over she tore into herself: *Why didn't I see this before? Why did I stay so long? Why didn't I see this coming?* Of course she bore some responsibility for what went wrong. Figuring out and maturely accepting your own responsibility is helpful. Flagellating yourself for real or perceived mistakes is not.

If the divorce seems sudden, you're probably asking yourself: *Why? Why? Why did this happen?* You're bound to question what you thought your marriage was, says Carpenter. *Were we as strong as I thought? Why did you fall out of love with me?* The person who's surprised often wonders if she ever had a solid grasp of reality. Was *anything* really true?

Some people assume if you've been together a long time, you should have seen your problems ages ago. But we're so invested in our marriages, in certain truths and myths, that very few in your place would have seen more or done better.

Use Your Anger to Help Yourself; Let It Go Before It Destroys You

Anger often emerges after your initial shock and grief. Some feel it immediately, like this sixty-five-year-old man. "She dumped me," he seethes, explaining how his wife left him when he was most down, out of a regular job and processing the death of two close family members. He felt "betrayed," even as he mourned the lost future he'd imagined for them. *How did my life get so fucked up?* he asked himself.

Anger can drive you even if *you* asked for the divorce. After all, no one does this without provocation. Pamela* did it after nineteen years of marriage to a kind but emotionally distant man. He spent almost every waking hour working. In couples therapy, he said he was happy in the marriage; she was the one with the problem. Pressed to make changes, he made none. When she finally told him she was done and moved into her own place, sadness and anger overwhelmed her before the joy of liberation.

"We never fought," she says, "but there was a total absence of love, affection, and communication. Our kids thought that was normal. I felt *angry* that he neglected me for so long, that he never fought for me in therapy or would do *anything* to keep me."

Many people, especially women, have to work to unearth their anger. Do it. It's often a potent antidote to depression and self-blame. But be careful. While anger can be a powerful friend, it can also burden you with misery.

When Patty's husband of seventeen years admitted he'd been unfaithful, he asked for a divorce. Her world was shaken, her sense of self blown apart. She'd worked as a writer and massage therapist, but her main focus had been on being his wife. As he rose to success in the entertainment industry, she threw the lavish parties for him and made their life run. "I'd created my entire identity around being his wife," she says. "My sense of value as a person, wife, woman was tied only into his opinion of me. As he made more money, his emotional abuse slowly ate away at my value. He'd deny me my feelings, telling me I was oversensitive."

When he told her he wanted a divorce, her initial feelings were shock, disbelief, and panic. Anger took a long time to emerge. Her parents' constant fighting made her believe that anger was unhealthy *and* not "ladylike." So she turned her anger inward. She slept around. She drank to numb her pain. Three months after the breakup, she attempted suicide.

Friends stepped in. One moved in with her for a time; another called often. After about a year, she began searching for ways to get better. "I immersed myself in every healing practice, book, seminar, audio program, and practice I discovered," she says. "I took walks, threw rocks, purged belongings, meditated, postulated, and burned things ceremoniously."

But before she could confront her anger, she needed perspective. The first and most useful thing she did was practice gratitude, a tool I suggest for you. *I might be going through this*, she told herself, *but I have food, shelter, and people who love me. I have my health.*

From YouTube and books, she devoured inspirational stories of people who'd suffered far worse than she but made triumphant re-coveries. She was most moved by a TED Talk by Amy Purdy. Purdy had nearly died from an illness that cost her both legs, a kidney, and her hearing. Previously an avid snowboarder, she related how she'd survived it all and become a snowboarder again. "I must have watched it fifty times," Patty says. One reason she identified with Purdy was because they'd both been massage therapists.

She also volunteered in a soup kitchen, getting into a comforting rhythm of cutting vegetables that reminded her of the cooking she'd done joyfully for the many parties she'd given during her marriage.

During this period, anger flared up in bits and snatches. She read books about anger and understood far more than she'd taken in from her parents' experiences. "I grasped that it's unhealthy to sup-press it or numb it," she says. She knew she had to feel it in order to heal, but she was afraid of her anger, afraid it would be perma-nent. She let herself rage while she dug in her garden. She punched pillows and screamed at an empty chair where she imagined her husband sat.

Based on her mother's example, Patty knew the most important thing about anger: to let it go and move on. "My mom held on to her anger and bitterness and never recovered," she says. "I was determined to not let this defeat me."

Around this time, she began life-coach training and learned tools that would help her and ultimately others get through heartbreak. She shares many of these on her website, PattyBlueHayes.com.

How to Find Your Anger, Express It, and Let It Go

If you can't feel your anger, make a list of things your spouse did that made you unhappy or undermined your marriage. Include unpleasant things you no longer have to do, from seeing his mother to picking up his dirty socks.

- *Express your anger safely.* When we first discover our suppressed anger, it sometimes explodes into irrational rage. Release this pent-up fury when you're alone or with someone safe, so you won't hurt yourself or anyone else. Scream out violent thoughts, uncensored, while you hit a pillow. Rage silently while thwacking a ball against a wall or stampeding down a running path or whatever does it for you. Repeat as needed.
- *Apply logic to your anger.* This is important and *hard*. When anger overwhelms you, you're probably not thinking clearly. Cognitive behavioral therapy (CBT) can help. I learned this practice in therapy, and I find it explained clearly in psychologist

Seth J. Gillihan's book *Cognitive Behavioral Therapy Made Simple: 10 Strategies for Managing Anxiety, Depression, Anger, Panic, and Worry* and *The CBT Workbook for Perfectionism: Evidence-Based Skills to Help You Let Go of Self-Criticism, Build Self-Esteem, and Find Balance* by Sharon Martin and Julie de Azevedo Hanks. There are also other good books on CBT you can find on your own.

Which thoughts and beliefs make you angry? Write them down. Now check them out for logical holes in your thinking. These are common ones:

- *Thinking in black and white.* If you think, for example, *My spouse is a horrible person who ruined a good marriage,* you're not seeing the shades of responsibility you each bear. When you identify your own role—and I'll help you do that— you'll understand this thought can't be true.
- *Believing things should be different from the way they are.* We all do this. When we dislike what is, we believe it *should* be different; it should be the way we *wish* it were. *He should have come home from work more. She should have wanted sex more. He should have been more financially responsible. She should have been a better mother.* Being angry for how things are makes no sense and gets you nowhere.
- *Minimizing the positive.* This is similar to black-and-white thinking. When we're emotional, we tend to discount the positive parts of our marriage. *He never loved me! She ruined every vacation we ever took. He did nothing to save our marriage. He never thought about the children.* Thinking like this stirs

up fury, which we may prefer to feeling the pain of the good things we've lost.

Think back over your marriage. Remember the good times, some lovely things your ex did. Write these down. Read them to help you see your marriage more realistically.

- *Having a distorted view of power or powerlessness.* When we blame ourselves for everything, we tell ourselves we have more power than we can possibly have. Think of a child who believes *Daddy got sick because I was mad at him.* Just as fallacious (and harmful) is believing we're helpless with no power at all. Feeling powerless can make you rage. If you've ever seen a three-year-old shrieking because he has to leave the playground, you'll know what that looks like. You may not have been able to prevent your divorce, but you have lots of power over how you behave, how you feel, and how you will live now.

Acknowledge Your Role in the End of Your Marriage

Once your anger cools, you can begin to see *your* part in your breakup. This is often the last and one of the hardest steps in healing.

Start with this idea. Every marriage has two people in it. Each one plays a role in how the marriage works. There is no such thing as a failed marriage where only one person was responsible. You can blame yourself for picking this partner or for staying in the marriage so long. That's not the same as thinking about the dynamics of your marriage and identifying your role. If you haven't done this, you haven't fully healed. And you're susceptible to making similar mistakes.

"There's virtually always a way we contribute," says Connecti-
cut marriage and family therapist Jill Whitney. "It may be through
silence, a tone that exacerbates an issue, or being overly critical. It
may be your not asserting yourself or stifling your partner. Maybe
when your partner grows, you're not willing to take risks to grow
yourself."

Maxi,* a psychotherapist in her mid-fifties, was devastated when
Sarah* asked for a divorce. "Traumatized with intense grief" is how
she describes it. Because Maxi was estranged from her parents,
Sarah, her wife of twelve years, had *been* her family. So when their
marriage ended, Maxi found refuge with loving friends. She pulled
herself together to work with her patients, and she took comfort in
seeing that she could help them despite her own misery.

Between appointments, she blasted Des'ree through her headphones:

> *You gotta be bad, you gotta be bold, you gotta be wiser*
> *You gotta be hard, you gotta be tough, you gotta be stronger*

Eventually, she realized how she and Sarah had each played a
part in sabotaging their relationship. Having married at almost forty,
Sarah was intent on having a baby. Maxi agreed. Round after round of
fertility treatments failed. After several years, Maxi agreed to try with
her eggs, but she was not really comfortable doing it or even with the
idea of parenthood.

Maxi enrolled in social work school to become a therapist: "That
was *my* baby," she says. When Sarah tried to get Maxi's attention to
look at sperm donors, she'd participate negligently. "She was angry,
blaming me," Maxi says. "I was withholding."

For Kevin,* about fifty, accepting his responsibility took time. It
was easy to blame his immature wife. Even though they'd broken up,

he'd married her when he'd learned she was pregnant. His friends begged him not to: The two were completely incompatible.

But once married, he tried valiantly to make it work. To placate her, he even agreed to an open marriage. They had three kids, and they fought constantly. Since she knew he hated her having tattoos, whenever she was angry with him, she got another one. Still, when she asked for a divorce, he was shaken and appalled. "I felt sad and angry at her abandoning our family unit," he says, even while a part of him saw a chance at freedom.

At first he took the blame. "I could have been a better person," he says. Then he began looking at his marital behavior more thoughtfully. "I made decisions along the way that went against what I thought was right, like bringing someone else into our bed. It's not good if you want an intimate relationship. I was raised Catholic and I wasn't even living a Christian marriage." He knows now that he should have asserted himself more or left the marriage sooner.

He feels good that he never vilified her. He accepts that they each bear responsibility.

How to Identify Your Role in Your Divorce

While it may temporarily comfort you to believe that you are the morally superior person to whom a great wrong was done, this posture won't heal you. To grow emotionally, work to understand your own part. That's your path to a happier future.

Do these exercises. Think hard and be brutally honest with yourself if that's what it takes.

Exercise 1

Write down four or five core areas in your relationship that did not work well. For example:

- How often you had sex, who initiated it, what it was like
- How you did or did not resolve conflict
- How you managed your financial life
- How you did or did not show affection, physically or verbally
- How you spoke to each other
- How you handled issues involving family members

Think about each issue separately. Write what the problem was for you and what it was for your partner. How did you behave? How did your ex behave? What was the effect of your part? Your ex's part? Was there any way or any time when you could have handled this differently or better? How? When? Ask yourself: *Did I do anything to make it worse, including doing nothing? How did my behavior make my* partner *feel?*

Ask yourself: *Why did I react this way? Mistaken beliefs? Reactions built in from childhood? Fears? Imitation of my parents' behaviors?* (See the next section.) *How might I behave differently in a new relationship?*

After you've written this out, put it aside for a while, then take it out and review it. Have you thought of anything else? Is there anything you'd like to change? Have any feelings changed as you've reapportioned responsibility for your breakup?

Exercise 2

Now that you've *thought* about your marital life from both sides, imagine how your ex *feels*. This is an exercise that I've seen get powerful results.

Set two chairs opposite each other. Sit in one and imagine your ex is in the other. Speak or yell or cry what you feel. Vent your grievances. Express your hurts. Ask your questions: Why, why, why? Try to limit yourself to one issue at a time, then move to the other chair. You are now your ex. Respond as this person you know so well, whom you lived with so long. Answer the questions, react to the complaint or hurt. Try as hard as you can to respond as he or she might have done.

Then move to your chair and be yourself again. Answer back. Switch chairs. Keep doing this as long as you feel you're learning something or until you feel you've reached a stopping place for now.

Repeat this exercise over time. You'll get better at it. You'll learn new things. You may even come to feel compassion for the one you once loved. That will help you feel compassion for yourself.

Your Role: Look to Your Parents'
Marriage (and Divorce) for Clues

As I heard story after story of relationships gone awry, I was struck by how often people used their parents' marriage as a reference point. Some had replicated it unconsciously. One fifty-seven-year-old divorcée, for example, mentioned that her parents were often sarcastic with each other, a clear sign of unaddressed resentment. She believed husband and wife should not fight. Maybe the ideal of their marriage—well, the myth—was that a wife's job was to please her husband: Put on makeup every night, make him feel good about himself, keep *him* comfortable and happy.

Others observed their parents' marriage and resolved never to be like them. Yet the partners they picked inevitably resembled one or both of their parents. What they expected about love often reflected their parents' relationship as well as how their parents showed *them* love.

Dorothy, for example, vowed *not* to become a wife like her mother. Her father had arrived in the United States unable to speak English and unable to support his family. His wife heaped him with scorn and rage, turning to daughter Dorothy to meet her needs. Feeling suffocated, the adult Dorothy sought an entirely different kind of marriage. "I wanted to marry a man whose forceful personality could reassure me that I would not become like her. I was looking for someone whom I could think of not as an equal, but as someone I could admire as smarter and more accomplished than I was."

That goal was a recipe for disaster. She married a man she describes as "a charismatic, alcoholic novelist." She imagined herself as his muse and that the two of them were one. She found that they were: He was that one. There was no room for her. She thought she'd avoided her parents' marriage. In fact, she'd chosen a similarly unequal relationship, but with her in the subservient role.

Another woman married a man who couldn't possibly be like her abusive father, with his volcanic temper. Her husband was a kind, quiet man who never said a harsh word. Twenty years later, she was horribly lonely. She realized that, like her father, her husband was emotionally unavailable, incapable of intimate companionship or warmth.

This stuff is *complicated*. Yet examining your parents' marriage can offer clues to the dynamics of your own and the part *you* played in it.

If your parents divorced, find your way back to your experience of it. If you were a child, you may not have known how to process this family cataclysm; it may still be reverberating and intensifying the pain of your own breakup. One fifty-four-year-old divorcée, for example, unearthed the wounded thirteen-year-old she'd been when her parents split up. At a weekend retreat harnessing art and meditation among other therapeutic tools, she remembered the last night in her childhood home. The house was empty; the furniture waited outside for the movers' van. She was to live with her father. She remembers perching on a chair, shivering in the cold. In her fifties, these feelings were still inside her. "I was afraid, grief-stricken," she says. "I felt the loss of family, abandonment, and isolation. I felt untethered and insecure."

Until she recovered these memories, she'd never felt fully healed from her own divorce despite lots of progress. "I never correlated that my divorce would bring up these feelings from childhood," she says. Having finally confronted them, she could grieve as an adult and lay these painful shadows to rest.

As you analyze your parents' marriage, though, bear in mind that the way they showed love to each other is probably the way they showed love to you. That's the love that feels most familiar. For example, if your father showed his love by being a good provider and buying you things, that may be what attracted you when you married. If your mother loved you by fretting over your inadequacies, your spouse may have done the same. The more you learn about yourself, your past and present needs, the better prepared you'll be to find the life partner you want now.

Put Your Parents' Marriage Under the Microscope

Think of your parents as a couple, not as your parents. Look back and observe them as if you were an astute friend. Ask yourself these questions, and try to go beyond your first knee-jerk reactions.

- What were the good things in their marriage? Affection? Mutual Respect? Friendship?
- Did they touch each other often? Laugh together? Appear (looking back, to your adult eyes) to have a good sex life?
- What were the less healthy things in their marriage?
- Did they build each other up or tear each other down?
- How did they resolve conflicts? Did one of them have more power and make more decisions? Did they yell? Talk quietly?
- Did they share responsibilities in an equitable way? What about finances?
- Did they parent well together or undermine each other's parenting?
- Was one seen as more dependent?
- Did either squelch the other's free expression out of fear of disapproval or anger?
- What advice did they give you about relationships? These, for example, are bits of parental "wisdom" women told me they heard from their mothers:

  Pick a man who loves you more than you love him.
  Don't ever be dependent on a man.

> *Your job as a wife is to make your husband happy, what-*
> *ever it takes.*
> *It's just as easy to love a rich man as a poor man.*
>
> Think about how your parents' advice may be flawed. Think hard
> about what you learned from them about marriage. What would you
> need to change to have a better relationship next time?

Don't Be a Victim

Your spouse may have been villainous, abusive, narcissistic, dishonest, or maybe all of the above. You chose this partner probably long
ago, when you were younger and less wise. You have another choice
now: to live as a perpetual victim or to move on to a happier life.

Make no mistake. There are perverse satisfactions to feeling vic-
timized. Retired North Carolina divorce attorney and twice-divorced
husband James Gray Robinson would ask his clients: "Do you want to
be happy or do you want to be right?" He says, "Inevitably, they would
want to be right. People who want revenge and to prove the other is
a bad person don't understand the emotional pain they will have to
suffer to achieve their goal."

When you see yourself as a victim, you envision yourself as the
hero of a tragic romantic drama, maybe like Anna Karenina, who
throws herself under a train. You feel anger, fear, hopelessness, and
loathing. That's your life.

Instead, think of where you are now as a doorway into a new and
better life. Imagine yourself as a caterpillar undergoing a (painful)
metamorphosis into someone stronger and happier. Robinson says

that his own two divorces taught him this. "If I looked for the posi-tives, the emotional pain was reduced."

Recognize that you're free from many constraints you had when you were younger, says British therapist Russell Thackeray. "You can develop a range of people who can offer different aspects of a great relationship rather than having to depend on one person," he says. "You can work out the relationships you want with family and friends and begin to live life on your terms.

"I see numerous examples of people in their fifties seeing divorce as an opportunity: doing things that their partner disapproved of," Thackeray says. "These include a wide array of self-expressions: run-ning a first marathon at sixty, vying for political office, coming out finally as gay."

List the Great Things You Can Do Now

To help you envision a positive future, keep a journal where you write down everything you can think of, however trivial or unlikely, that's newly possible.

You might include:

- Spend tranquil time thinking my own thoughts.
- Do anything I want without being second-guessed.
- Pick people I *want* to spend time with.
- Enjoy a satisfying sex life.
- Be with people who encourage and nurture me.
- Take French classes and go to Paris.
- Become a vegetarian.

- Manage my own finances and spend what I want on what I want.
- Decorate my own home and make it comfortable for *me*.

First and last on your list might be: Find a relationship in which I can be my best self and be happy.

One Journey from Divorce Trauma to New Love: What Worked for Trish Can Work for You

For Trish,* a sixty-four-year old midwestern business owner, a year of therapy came first. Following her divorce, she needed help healing from a kind of marital PTSD. After years of a lively dating life, at thirty-five, she'd married Ned.* The forty-one-year-old southern charmer had swooped her up, proposed within three months, and married her within six. He was attractive, brilliant, romantic, and exciting.

Once they were engaged, he revealed he was bipolar, and he suggested she call his psychiatrist. The doctor recommended several books about the disorder. She read them, but, she says, nothing prepared her for what their life would be like.

Like many people in love, she probably gleaned from those books just what she wanted to know. The one she remembers was by a high-functioning bipolar man who seemed to her a kind of "dark poet."

The oldest of four siblings, Trish had been a "twenty-four/seven babysitter," especially after her father's near-fatal heart attack when she was a teen and her mother had to support the family. Trish absorbed the idea that the younger ones' needs (everybody's needs, in fact) took precedence over her own. She also saw herself as the only introvert in the family. "Everyone else was screaming and taking what they wanted," she says. Not Trish. She was the responsible, competent one, a "can-do" person. She responded to Ned's illness as a challenge. "I was very naive," she says. "I thought, *I can fix things; I can make him a good life.*"

Many things about their marriage were wonderful. In the way her father adored her mother, Ned lavished attention on Trish, gifts and flowers. He had exquisite southern manners and charm. He'd listen to her. He'd take care of her in ways large and small, for example, filling her car with gas before she even knew she was running low. When she asked him to join her marketing business, he gave up his plans to go to engineering school. He seemed smart and competent; he was older and projected confidence. She trusted him and relied on him.

Five years in, she knew she wasn't happy, but she ignored the warning signs. She always had to beg for sex (she blamed his medication for his lack of desire). Over time, their sex life withered to nothing. His temper became ferocious. With what she calls a "Tony Soprano–style of reprimand," he created a reign of terror at work, setting off a drain of good employees. He criticized and judged her constantly, keeping her in a constant state of anxiety that she'd done something wrong.

Yet she stayed with him for ten years. She's asked herself why a thousand times. Her explanation is that their marriage was "about fifty/fifty terribleness and awesomeness." It was similar to "battered wife syndrome," she explains. He'd "beat" her verbally, then beg for forgiveness: "I'll do anything for you. I have this terrible illness I can't control." He'd then devote himself to pleasing and adoring her, until the next outburst. Her oversize sense of responsibility also weighed on the side of staying with him. *I married this person,* she told herself, *I have to do it.*

Near the end, Ned's doctor took him off lithium, which no longer worked. She shuttled him back and forth to medical appointments as each new medication failed. She felt more like a caregiver than a wife. She joked to herself that her saintly behavior would win her a special place in heaven.

At this point, he told her the marriage was too stressful for him; he wanted a divorce. He also spat out that he just didn't like her anymore. Despite how awful much of their marriage had been, she was plunged into grief. For many months, she missed him and mourned their marriage.

Soon sadness gave way to practical crises. All along, his huge confidence had led her to undervalue her own convictions about how to run the business. After he left, she found out he'd leased equipment they didn't need and couldn't afford. When government notices started arriving, she discovered he hadn't submitted their payroll taxes for years. He'd also maxed out their credit cards. She was deeply in debt.

While she coped with this ghastly reality, she was beset by flashbacks and nightmares. She'd walk into rooms frantic about whether she'd deposited her checks, one of many things he'd made her feel judged and anxious about.

She pursued healing through three paths. First, in therapy she searched for insight into their respective roles in what she told herself was "a waste of the last fifteen years." At her therapist's suggestion, she made a list of all the negative things she no longer had to do for him. As the list grew to nearly a hundred items, from doing his laundry to making excuses to people for his horrible behavior, she began getting angry. "The number and nature of the things were shocking to me," she says. "This got me to the anger stage faster. Now I advise all newly divorced people I know to try this—ha!"

For several years, however, her internal angry "tape" alternated with a tape of regret, pity, guilt, and self-blame: *Why didn't I heed the warning signs? Why did I stay so long? I'm so stupid. I'm a sucker. Why couldn't I make it work? Why did I let him second-guess me?*

After a year of therapy, she quit, feeling she'd learned all she could.

She still found life punishing. "Every day I felt hopeless and used up as a functioning human being," she says. Then, five years after the divorce, she awoke one morning, sputtering out loud, "He was a really bad husband!" She'd finally broken through the self-blame to the anger she needed. Those tapes stopped circling in her head.

The second and concurrent track of healing was rebuilding her business. Bit by bit, she repaired the damage, salvaged clients, and struck out in new directions. Whenever she made a successful move, she told herself, *I knew I had good instincts. Why did I listen to him?*

The third track of becoming whole was caring for herself in ways not possible during her marriage: She visited old college friends around the country who made her feel loved. She threw herself into hobbies like sewing and metalsmithing. She traveled to Europe and Asia. A self-confessed "emotional eater," she lost fifty-five pounds and joined a gym.

After about five years, she had epiphanies about her role in the failure of the marriage. These perceptions sputtered up in fragments until she could finally articulate the mistakes she'd made. One of the earliest was insisting that Ned give up the idea of graduate school to become her business partner. "Couples shouldn't work together," he'd said. But her parents had worked together and were the happy couple she wished to be. As her business grew, she says, "he finally capitulated, and both of us were miserable."

Because she had trouble standing up to him, she realizes now, she did destructive passive-aggressive things. For example, he lived beyond their means on the company credit cards and got angry if she tried to stop him. To curb his access to money, Trish would "forget" to deposit checks into their account. Ned's checks would bounce. "It was all-out war and finger-pointing," she says.

One big mistake, she says, was this: "I didn't state my needs and beliefs on the important issues, and I tried to carry a hundred and ten percent of the responsibility to fix all the problems in the relationship."

When Trish's girlfriends saw her newly svelte, happily occupied, and no longer angry, they decided she was ready to date. She agreed to try it as a lark. She had a yearlong relationship with a man who adored her and was a great lover. "He gave me back my joy of life," she says. On the minus side, he was a "big baby." He pouted when she couldn't see him because her mother had a health crisis. She broke it off.

Afterward she felt ready for a serious relationship. She thought hard about the kind of partner she wanted. On her long list were kind, supportive, and "no drama."

She is now six years into that relationship. She and her partner live together. They keep their finances totally separate. She says, "I love him, but I have no problem drawing my lines in the sand with him."

How to Move Forward if You've Been Widowed

Like divorced people, you must grieve and remake your identity. Yet losing a partner to death is different. Grief can overwhelm your life. Healing takes time, and every loss is different.

How you move forward depends on many things. Was your partner's death expected or sudden? Were you a caregiver for a spouse suffering a long, wasting illness? Was your marriage relatively happy? Or do you suffer anger and guilt after a conflicted marriage? If the latter, you may suffer what therapists call "complicated grief." It will probably last longer, and you may need professional help to fully sort out your feelings.

For some, healing is fairly straightforward. If you're older, if the death was expected, if the marriage was fairly good, you will hurt but also take comfort from what you had. Family and friends can support you, but there's no substitute for time: time to hurt, to mourn, to observe anniversaries with the acute pain of loss and remembrance of joy. Eventually, you will emerge on the other side.

For others, and I am one, healing was not simple. When Alan died, I was shocked and devastated but not surprised. I believe he died of denial, mainly his own but also mine. Besides the anguish of *losing* him, I also felt anger, guilt, regret, and confusion.

The short version is that he died of a heart attack. The full story is that he'd been told he needed to have an aortic valve replaced. He was frightened of doctors, terrified of giving up control to anyone else. He worried he would die on the operating table. There were risks to the surgery, of course, but his were not high.

His father had this same operation in his sixties. In his late forties, Alan convinced himself if he moved cautiously, he could delay the surgery for a couple of decades. He researched his condition. He read medical journals. He trusted in the parts that fit with his theory and ignored the rest.

I begged him to see a cardiologist. I told him he was irresponsible to risk leaving our two young daughters fatherless. I finally persuaded him. He brought along a five-page closely written "brief" arguing why he could put off the operation. When that cardiologist and a second one were unconvinced, he found another doctor who agreed he could wait six months and then be reexamined.

Nothing I said could ever get him to go back. He delayed and delayed. I talked to a friend's brother who was a cardiologist. He told me that anyone with Alan's symptoms who didn't have the valve replaced would be dead within three years. I told Alan. He still didn't go back. Nothing I said made any difference. I gave up and hoped he was right.

Of course he wasn't. One night he collapsed in our bedroom. "Should I call 911?" I screamed. "No!" he said. He quickly stood up. "It's just a bad flu." He swore he'd go to the doctor in the morning. When he did, the doctor sent him right to the hospital. As he lay on an examining table, he answered the doctors' questions with evasions. No, he hadn't had chest pains, he said.

"Don't lie to them," I shouted, "or they can't help you." He admitted maybe he'd had chest pains. His condition was critical, the doctors told me. They admitted him and worked furiously to save him. A few hours later, they came out to the waiting room, shaking their heads sadly. When I walked outside and down the seemingly endless flight of hospital steps, an image I still carry with me, I felt numb. My whole life had changed in an instant.

After the funeral gatherings and observances, I was alone with my daughters. I often shut the solid wood door to my bedroom while I wept and keened and screamed into a pillow. Now I understood what people meant when they said they felt as if an arm had been cut off. As time passed, I felt anger. His was a totally preventable death. He had done this to himself, to us. I also felt stinging guilt. If I had only called 911! If only I'd *insisted* he have the operation!

Over time, I scrutinized my guilt. Suppose I'd called 911. Alan might have refused to get in the ambulance. A year before, when he blacked out on the street, fell on his face, and broke his jaw, he ran away when he saw the ambulance someone had called. I found him bloody at home. He insisted he had just tripped.

This was a man determined to avoid the operation. He was my husband and I loved him. But he was a separate human being with his own will. I could not substitute my will for his.

Over time my anger faded. After all, I was alive and still able to enjoy our children and my friends and a whole new life I could create as I wished. He was not. I pictured how he used to sing ruefully that line from "Margaritaville": "Some people claim that there's a woman to blame / But I know it's my own damn fault."

Other widowed people suffer anger, guilt, and regret. One woman, widowed as she turned sixty, was consumed by guilt at first. Her husband, older by fifteen years, had had a heart condition for years and done everything he could to stay healthy. Yet she reproached herself: She should have been home the day he died!

Now, years later, she says she thinks that even if she'd been there, she might not have been in the room when he died. "He came to me in dreams," she says. "I felt he'd forgiven me, and I had to forgive myself." Looking back, she muses, "What's the point of holding on to this? I had to let go."

Like me, she joined a bereavement group. Being with others mourning loss helped her make sense of it. The support of her long-time yoga group also helped her. "I started yoga teacher training," she says. "My heart was so empty, I needed to fill it with something, and it did fill my heart."

The steps we took are available to you. But, widowed or divorced, if you want to move on to a new love, you must first rediscover yourself as a single person.

Start in small ways by having experiences you didn't share with your partner. Buy something new, a dish towel that he never saw, a set of super-masculine sheets she'd have hated. When my dear friend Donna bought me gorgeous silver earrings from Georg Jensen on my first birthday after Alan's death, I said, "Donna, I don't have pierced ears."

"So get them pierced," she shot back. "It will be a sign of your new life."

So I did, and so it was.

Re-Create Yourself as a Single Person

When you've been long partnered, a big part of your identity is being half of a couple. Newly single, you're likely to ask: *Who am I now?* "Take time to establish your sense of self," says Villanova University psychology professor Erica Slotter.

Start with what you *must* do: Take on responsibilities your partner used to handle, whether you're figuring out your own taxes or doing the yard work. For one new divorcée who feared being unable to manage on her own, both these tasks turned out to be doable and gave her a new sense of confidence in arenas she'd never considered part of her identity before. "Mastering the Weed Wacker was my big triumph," she told me with a laugh years later, when she was happily remarried. Many newly single people, partly out of necessity, many out of passion, devote themselves to a new career or avocation.

As half of a couple, you may have compromised on what you liked, where you vacationed, what you ate. One divorced woman shared an epiphany: She and her husband had their first marriage counseling session, during which the therapist asked: "Are you here to save your marriage or end it?" "Save it!" she said emphatically as her husband declared, "End it." Reeling with shock as they left, she noticed the therapist's furniture and thought, *If I'm not with him, why do I have a house filled with mission furniture? I don't even like mission furniture.* It was a tiny but important first step in resurrecting who she used to be and creating who she would become.

To help you learn who the new single *you* can be, consider which things you'd like to keep, which new things you might want to add.

- What things did I enjoy as part of a couple? What things as an individual? If you wanted to travel but couldn't, plan a trip now. If you want to see foreign films, do it!
- Make a list of qualities you'd like to develop. Physical bravery? Take a trapeze class or join a rock-climbing group.
- If you're widowed, think about qualities you loved in your late partner and, if possible, make them a part of yourself. It's a way both to accept your spouse's loss and to honor and keep her in your heart. One widow in her seventies, for example, had always been shy. She found that after all those years watching her sociable husband charm people, she'd learned how. Like him, she made eye contact with people, asked questions, listened. She easily formed new social circles as she tried new activities that hadn't interested him—cooking classes, for example, and anthropology.

Whether widowed or divorced, credit yourself for having come though one of life's hardest trials, and you can confront whatever comes your way. You've probably emerged from grief or depression with a renewed sense of strength and possibility. Harness it to move forward.

As you look ahead to dating, it's natural to feel both trepidation and desire. For the widowed, even thinking about a new relationship raises questions of identity. Tamara Statz, a Minnesota marriage and family therapist who specializes in older clients, works with many widowed people. Women in particular, she says, struggle with issues of identity:

> *I was a wife for most of my life. Who am I now?*
> *Am I single?*
> *Would my late spouse want me to be with someone else? Or*
> *   would it be a betrayal?*
> *Might I enjoy being on my own?*

"Moving from 'we' to 'I' can be meaningful and different. Give yourself permission to *think* about that," Statz advises. "It can be exciting even as it involves intense grief."

If you had the luxury of time while your partner was dying, you may have received permission, even encouragement, from your spouse, to find a new partner. The widow who took yoga teacher training tried to shush her husband when he referred to "your next husband." But she knew he wanted that for her. Eight years after his death, she's met a man she has let into her heart.

Chapter Two

Identify the Emotional Traits
of Your Next Partner

Most people in the dating world have firm ideas about what they're looking for. They have definite no-gos or deal-breakers. Good-to-haves might include qualities like bookish, outdoorsy, or musical. Most important, if you can identify them, are the emotional must-haves: empathic and emotionally stable, for example, nonjudgmental, flexible, and independent. These comprise your *conscious shopping list*.

You may also have an emotional agenda you're not aware of. If you're seeking perfection or unrealistic standards, you might be working against what you think you want and scuttling your search. In this chapter, I'll help you identify and evaluate both your conscious preferences and your hidden needs.

Focus on the Emotional *Traits*

After age fifty, life begins to change. Maybe you're still active, energetic, and adventurous, but you know time is not limitless. Your life is less about looking forward, forging a career, or raising a family. Parents pass on. Friends begin to die. You or those around you cope with chronic ailments. The glossy attributes of a prospective mate that once dazzled you no longer seem so relevant when your father is disappearing into the neverland of Alzheimer's or your daughter's oldest child is autistic. You live more in the present; your feelings are more nuanced and multidimensional. You experience joy tinged with bittersweet memories, sorrow leavened by joy. The loving mate you want by your side, people tell me, needs to be your emotional partner in the delights or trials of the rest of your life. Many smile at what they valued in their youth: someone good-looking, ambitious, wealthy, or well connected.

Maureen,* seventy-four, now married to Alastair,* sixty-nine, recalls how pressured she felt as a college senior to get married. "The universe didn't tell me I was capable of supporting myself," she says. "I had to find a husband." In her world, the prize was a doctor. Hooray, she won the prize. She and her doctor had a long, unhappy marriage. She was always deemed lesser. He never valued her or even the money she earned. "He was never nice to me," she recalls, "even when we were dating."

After divorcing him, she was single for years. When she started dating, she wanted to find someone who loved and *valued* her. She married Alastair in her fifties, and she basks in his affection and respect. "I used to want to go to fancy restaurants and parties. Now I just enjoy playing Scrabble at home with him or going grocery shopping together," she says.

Yet others—maybe you?—are still seeking those glossy credentials, says dating coach Sandy Weiner (LastFirstDate.com), who helps clients identify more substantial traits. For many, she says, "the person needs to be kind, have a good heart, be responsible and capable of commitment. Their list should focus on life skills rather than superficial qualities."

Justify Your Must-Haves — to Yourself

Try this exercise:

Write down everything you want in a partner. Frame the qualities positively: for example, "honest and trustworthy" instead of "not a cheater."

List your top ten. For each requirement, explain *why* you need it. Be as detailed as possible. For example, if you enjoy foreign travel, explain why having a partner who will accompany you is a must-have.

Then, as therapist Russell Thackeray suggests, read the list out loud and record it. Speak as if talking to a friend: "This is important to me because . . ." "I *need* this because . . ."

Now play back what you've recorded. When you *listen* to yourself justify the importance of a particular quality, Thackeray says, "you can hear when you are not confident, when you are stretching the truth. You can hear it in your voice, and you will know when you are lying to yourself."

Now rewrite the list, including only what you can justify as essential.

I'd like to tell you I focused on essentials when I started dating after Alan died. But I didn't. I yearned for excitement and passion and new experiences. Some of my like-to-have attributes were downright silly and changed from month to month. After my infatuation with a romantic, poem-writing pilot who turned out to be a no-goodnik, I added "pilot" to my nice-to-have list. I started noticing when guys mentioned they had planes. I even dated a few pilots. One was a nice guy, but no sparks (and no flying trips, either). Another was married. Some men I chose to meet were completely unlike others I'd known.

It was good for me to meet them, but if I wanted a serious relationship, my selection standards were foolish. With time, I started discriminating more, at least consciously.

If I'd been too open in picking people, I then became ridiculously narrow. I winnowed my prospects down to widowers with advanced degrees. I was prejudiced against divorced people because I assumed they had bad relationship skills and had "failed." Whatever issues Alan and I had (and we had plenty), we stayed together until his death did us part.

Because I live in densely packed Manhattan, I did find widowers with master's degrees or doctorates. I met several. Some obviously had been, from what they told me, terrible husbands. Two were consumed by guilt because they'd cheated on their wives (so much for my theory that widowers make better husbands). Another was determined to avoid any serious relationship because that would dishonor his late wife, whom he worshipped. A couple of others were nice guys but not on my wavelength.

So I opened up to divorced men. Some seemed to have learned a great deal from their breakups and looked like good relationship prospects, but not for me. I also met a few guys without college degrees who were smart and thoughtful. Another prejudice discredited.

Don't follow my example, at least not early on. Look at people like those below. Are their needs and life situations at all like yours?

One newly married woman in her fifties, for example, told me that at her stage of life, she needed someone stable, understanding, and supportive. Within months of their wedding, her husband proved himself to be all these, as she'd known he would. "I broke my leg and was in a cast for ten weeks," she says, grateful for how he cared for her. "He also saw me through the deterioration of my dad's health."

Another just-remarried woman in her fifties values the steadiness of her husband over the "wildness and excitement" she craved in her youth. "What's important to me now is having a safe place to fall, knowing he has my back all the time," she says.

What's right for you? That depends on your current life situation, your *understanding* of what you need, and what did and did not work in your previous relationships.

Leanne,* for example, a divorced woman in her early sixties, enjoyed a several-year relationship with a passionate Frenchman, but she knew he would not be a good lifetime partner. "He had never been married or had kids; he wanted me just for himself," she says. "I knew when I became a grandma, his jealousy and possessiveness would not work." After she ended it with him, she met a stable family man who was close to his own children and grandchildren. He was intellectually more compatible, neither needy nor possessive. When they married, they created a life that allowed them both the time they wanted with their own families as well as intimacy with each other.

You may not be sure about your needs. Terri* wasn't. After a difficult marriage, making a better choice was her priority. To figure this out, she had to dig deep inside.

Approaching sixty, she was occupied by work and family responsibilities. She valued her independence and network of close friends. But she also wanted a partner. She worked on a list of the traits she needed in a new partner. Over several months, she added and subtracted and reprioritized them. Emotional stability topped her list (her ex had been unstable). Then came kindness, supportiveness, and contentment with himself and his life. Much farther down, she listed intellectual excitement and financial status, two items she'd valued highly when young.

As she studied what she'd written, she realized that an old boyfriend fit this model. She and Jack* had dated on and off in their twenties but drifted apart. She had loved him, sort of, but she couldn't see him as a life partner. Coming from an upper-middle-class background, Terri valued ambition. She wanted someone she could travel the world with. Jack came from a blue-collar family and was happy staying put and being who he was. "He was laid-back," she says, "not ambitious. In my twenties, I had plans. I wanted to backpack in Europe."

She asked around, found out Jack was single, and called him. They met for dinner and talked for hours. He was vulnerable, which she appreciated, and they both felt chemistry. He didn't have everything on her list, but he had enough. Five years later, they're living together. They feel grateful to have come together again at the *right* time. Jack has sustained her through her mother's decline. "He's very giving," she says, "and he 'gets' me." It's different from in their twenties. "We're both more emotionally supportive," she says. "Back then I was trying to fit him into my mold. I wanted Mr. Wall Street."

Ask Yourself: Which Needs Must My Partner Fill? Which Can I Look to Others to Satisfy?

Sure, you'd like your significant other to travel with you, hike or cycle with you, go to the theater with you. It'd be great if he'd be riveted when you analyze the issues your friend is having with her kid. But are all these *necessary*?

Many of the happy couples I interviewed don't look to each other for all their needs. A woman friend routinely travels to Europe with a group of other women whose husbands don't like to travel. A male friend goes on a kayaking trip to South America every year with friends from college. Some do day trips on their own with special-interest clubs.

Friends (or people in hobby or religious groups) can give you things you'd *like* from a partner. A woman who divorced a brilliant but abusive man told me she was so happy with her new mate, even though when they discussed books or the news, he didn't display the same brilliance as her ex. "I have plenty of friends who can give me intellectual stimulation," she says. "I don't need that from him."

Ask yourself: *What do I hope a significant other will do for me?* Write them down. Would your list be similar to this one?

1. to love and support me in difficult times
2. to give me affection
3. to have passionate sex with me
4. to help me feel better about myself
5. to make me feel more respected because I'm not single
6. to fill my time so I don't feel empty or bored
7. to be someone to do things with: see foreign films, eat in nice restaurants, go to concerts
8. to be cozy at home with
9. to listen and maybe offer suggestions as I struggle with problems
10. to watch the news and trade opinions with me

Now identify which needs you can—or *must*—satisfy yourself. If you feel internal needs like the fourth through sixth items, you may still need to do some headwork. These are holes no one can fill but you.

As health and fitness coach Debi Carlin Boyle, sixty-two, says, "When I married at age nineteen, I thought that you need another person to complete you." After her divorce thirty-five years later, she learned: "I had to get in my own lane." She learned to support herself, went back to school, and reinvented herself. She enjoyed living alone for the first time in decades. She took care of her own needs. She filled herself and her time with studying. She made friends with other single women and socialized, including on weekend trips. She enjoyed the emotional support and company of her two grown daughters.

Of course, you want a partner who's empathic and will listen to you, but you probably have friends who can do that, too, and who may know you better. As for activities, an online search will net you folks with whom you can do target shooting, visit museums, go rock climbing, or practice Italian conversation.

As therapist Krista Jarvis says, "When we fill ourselves up, learn to meet our own needs, and learn to cope with loneliness in ways that are fulfilling for us rather than destructive, we are much more apt to find a partner we can commit to out of love rather than fear. We are able to be patient and wait for the right companion for us."

Identify Traits That Did and Did Not Work in Your Previous Relationships

You're probably adamant about things you will never tolerate again. No narcissists! No addicts! No compulsive gamblers or problem drinkers! No _____: Fill in the blank! It's harder to recognize what was good in a failed relationship. But try.

All I knew after Alan died was that I wanted what I'd lacked with him: passion and excitement. I did not look for the kindness, trustworthiness, and supportiveness I so valued in him. So I fell for men who were infatuated with me at first sight and professed love in over-the-top ways. I wanted *romance*, and I found it, often to my sorrow.

With time, I got smarter. Others I spoke to were way ahead of my fifty-year-old self.

Ross* is a prime example. At age fifty-nine and devastated by an unexpected divorce, Ross focused entirely on the strengths he needed in his next and, he hoped, *last* partner. "I spent time alone learning about women, about pain, about myself," he says. "My faith played a big role." He knew he wanted a Christian woman who had children, solid values, a sense of humor, and high self-awareness. She had to be a woman who could stand on her own and not be needy, like his ex-wife.

When eHarmony suggested Melanie,* now his wife, they were incompatible by their friends' measures. He was seriously rich. She was a health care worker who lived on the wrong side of the tracks, and in their small southern town, these were literal railroad tracks.

Melanie was also seeking someone who shared "my faith, sense of humor, and love for family." What really sealed it for them was one item on the eHarmony questionnaire: *When you walk into a party with me, will you stay by my side or split off and mingle?* Both answered: *Mingle!*

Each insisted on creating a union of two independent and equal human beings, the sine qua non for true intimacy. When Ross said something that he intended to be gentlemanly, Melanie shot back, "I don't need a man to save me." Ross was thrilled. He didn't want a woman who needed saving, and he made her understand that. Despite the vast difference in their wealth, they agreed on basic values, such as giving to the less fortunate.

In her late sixties, Dorothy had also recognized true equality in a relationship as critical. After her terrible first marriage, she found that clarifying the kind of partner she needed was a long endeavor of trial and error and prioritizing. Her first husband had been a brilliant, self-centered man who kept her down. In the decades after her divorce, she had several relationships. From each, she learned what made her feel whole and healthy and what did not. Always thoughtful and introspective, she went into therapy, she read, she kept journals, and she talked to friends. All this taught her one critical lesson: In her past relationships, she had not felt good about *herself.*

At age sixty-eight, when Dorothy met Dan, she finally understood what she needed most. "I knew that I wanted to feel and be treated as an equal partner with neither of us dominating the other," she says. "I also knew I needed someone who was fundamentally decent, whose character I respected, someone I could count on to be there for me as I would be there for him." Readying herself for this, she says, "meant working on strengthening my emotional muscles of independence so I would not get myself into relationships that were unhealthy."

With Dan, she found all that as well as the brilliance and excitement that had always attracted her. Their relationship encouraged her to expand, to express herself more than ever before, and to like herself better in the relationship than she ever had. Those qualities were essential, whereas other things that she very much wanted were not. In fact, being with Dan required one important sacrifice.

Traveling in Europe was important to Dorothy. She was bilingual and had friends in Europe. Her background in literature deepened her overseas experiences and vice versa. She saw quickly that Dan would not share this with her. He did not enjoy the one trip to Europe they took, and he made it clear that he didn't want to do it again.

That was hard for Dorothy to accept, but she did. She weighed this disappointment against the feeling of being cherished that Dan gave her and what she called their "shared emotional intelligence." Ultimately she decided she'd rather stay home with him than go alone or with others. Ten years later, she says, "Not traveling together is a loss, but there are unsolvable problems in every relationship. This one was not a deal-breaker."

Beware of Choosing the Opposite Kind of Mate

It's a common mistake. If you had misery with your ex, you think the answer is to find someone completely opposite. This rarely works. After all, you were attracted to something in your ex. You might still want *some* of those qualities.

Richard, for example, an educator divorced in his late forties, had been drawn to his first wife because, as he says, "She was a risk-taker, adventurous, a bit iconoclastic." He'd been raised with solid middle-class values, to be realistic and grounded. "Being grounded can seem boring," he says. "The excitement of an edgy woman was the antidote to predictability and sameness."

After years of relative contentment, working and raising children, his wife developed serious signs of mental illness. "She would start therapy, and as soon as the therapist got through her facade, she would bail and find another," he recounts. He never found out whether she was suffering from depression or bipolar disorder, but she became fearful and reclusive, and the marriage ended.

After they divorced, Richard had a series of relationships in which he ping-ponged between opposites. His first girlfriend was attractive and stable but not intellectually stimulating or exciting. Next he was smitten with someone smart, attractive, and charismatic; he loved the adrenaline rush he got from her. After a year, he realized she was emotionally unstable and a liar. She'd told him, for example, that she was financially secure, a lie that was exposed as he watched the repo men haul away her car.

Reeling from this mistake, he found a stable older woman who was the opposite of the seductive liar. But the spark faded with time. In his late fifties, he craved adventure, like hiking in remote places. He saw his partner as rigid, unwilling to try new things. She didn't share his curiosity or energy.

Richard exemplifies why seeking the opposite of an ex, rather than a more complex and nuanced idea of a partner, doesn't work. Therapist Mark McGonigle says, "Reactivity, swinging from one extreme to the other, is not a stable ground for a relationship. If I'm with someone because of my reactivity to an old partner, those feelings are actually going to be there and destabilize the current relationship. The big question for me if I have been through a failed relationship is: What did I learn there? How can I take that into a place inside myself that's not reactive or judgmental but more understanding and compassionate?" It's hard to learn about yourself, he says, if you are constricted in your awareness by judgments about the other person and black-and-white thinking.

At this point, Richard says, he realized he needed to think more carefully. He saw that he needed *both* excitement and stability, someone emotionally secure but optimistic and joyful about life. When he met Anna, now his wife, he realized she was this perfect combination. For their relationship to work, however, he'd have to accept two things about her that he'd previously considered unacceptable. A bit later, I'll tell you how he overcame these stumbling blocks.

Figure Out What Did and Did Not Work in Your Previous Relationships

Make a chart of your important relationships (or the last five, if you've had many). Next to each person's name, write the qualities you enjoyed and would like again and the qualities or tendencies you want to avoid. Think hard in order to find positives as well as negatives for each. Even if the relationship ended badly, there were things you liked or loved about this person. What were they? What excited you? What made you feel good? What made you feel bad?

Ask yourself:

- What did I yearn for?
- What did I suffer that I never want to endure again?
- In that relationship, how did I feel about myself?
- How long did it last?
- How did it end?
- What was my part in its ending?

Do you see any patterns? For example, did you have to suppress parts of yourself to keep your partner happy? Did one of you always have to take care of the other?

With these patterns in mind, review your criteria for a partner. Ask yourself:

- What psychological attributes are *not* a match for me? (For example, if your spouse was kind of a teacher to you, do you want that again?)
- What are my values—about, for example, morality, money, and family? Must my partner share them all?
- What is my outlook about health and aging? Is it important that my partner share it? For Dorothy, it meant someone "whose awareness of being mortal includes a more intense appreciation of the present." You may feel that you are in what Erik Erikson called the generativity stage of life, when it's important to you to mentor the younger generation.

Give Your List a Reality Check

Try this exercise:

Write down your requirements for a partner. For example: youthful in spirit, smart, empathic, flexible, communicative, financially stable, athletic, charity-minded, well-organized, neat, culturally sophisticated, funny, etc. Next to each, use a numerical scale, from 1 to 5, to indicate how much this trait matters to you.

Now use your scale to rate yourself on each. Be honest. Then show it to a friend. Use your friend's input to rate yourself more accurately. If there are big disparities between your own positives and those you're seeking, something is off. You don't have to match on every category, and complementary traits can mesh well, but your criteria should reflect reality. It is in reality that you will find your true partner.

If you refuse to compromise on your must-haves, despite how much you say you want it, chances are that you're at least ambivalent about being in a relationship. Let's face it: Relationships bring risk. When you begin to care about someone, you make yourself vulnerable to hurt. If you've had painful experiences in the past, you may find an actual relationship too scary.

It's safer to long for your ideal, much as we did in high school. I was the plump, nerdy bookworm pining after the gorgeous class president. You may have been the freshman dreaming about the prom queen or the captain of the football team. Those crushes were *safe*. We were never going to date those people so out of reach. Are you a sixty-seven-year-old man of middling income, education, and talents, and your must-haves add up to a brilliant, successful career woman of forty? Then you're setting yourself up for failure. Aiming for "perfect" usually ends in zero.

If your "shopping list" includes many must-haves and many no-gos, please reconsider. If you say you're not willing to "settle," look deeper into yourself. No one wants a relationship that's unfulfilling or hurtful. But "settle" is a term people often use to give being realistic a bad name.

A Tale of Two Lists: What It May Tell You About Yours

Dennis* is a seventy-two-year-old health care professional in suburban Philadelphia. Gregory* is sixty-nine, a retired city official in Manhattan. Both are sensitive, thoughtful men who took responsibility for the failure of their respective relationships. They'd worked on themselves to become better partners. Each had recently been in a several-year relationship that fizzled.

Gregory had dated online for most of the eighteen years since his divorce. Dennis was trying it for the first time. Both had carefully worked out their list for a potential partner.

Dennis's was fairly short. He wanted a professional woman who'd provide the intellectual heft he'd found lacking in his most recent girlfriend. The women "had to be compatible with my guidelines," he says. "They needed to appear in their profiles like stable people with stable family relationships." For that reason, he liked when they posted photos with their grandkids. Most of all, he studied the body language in the photos. He wanted people who gave off warmth and positive energy.

He identified three women who met these criteria. He made three dates over the course of a long weekend: a coffee date on Saturday, a lunch date on Sunday, and drinks on Monday. In her profile, the first woman looked attractive and had positive body language. He set up a meeting even though she was not professional but "semi-professional." Also, she'd never been married, a "red flag" for him. Still, he was willing to judge her in person. The problem on their date turned out to be neither of these concerns. "She talked nonstop," he says. "I couldn't wait to get away from her."

When he got home from Date One, he had a message from Date Three, explaining that she was canceling because she'd realized she wasn't ready to date. He was disappointed. But he was still looking forward to Sunday lunch with Maggie,* a teacher. In all her photos, she showed good posture and "a light-up-the-room smile." She glowed. "She intrigued me," he says.

Their lunch lasted three hours. "We had so much in common," Dennis says. "She seemed like an intelligent and positive person." He asked to see her again, and again they really connected. On their third date, he received a call from his daughter-in-law telling him that his son had been in a serious accident and might be paralyzed. "Having heard my voice on the phone, [Maggie] *felt* what I was going through," he says. "She immediately reacted so positively, offering to help in any way she could."

For weeks, while he was away by his son's bedside, she called him every day to ask how he and his son were doing. His son recovered. Dennis and Maggie's relationship flourished. When I last spoke to him, they were engaged.

Gregory was less successful. After years on several dating sites, he had fine-tuned his list. She had to be very attractive (although he admits to being of "average" attractiveness himself). She had to be affectionate, passionate, and intellectual. She had to be physically fit (ten to twelve years younger, he says) and outdoorsy. She had to be adventurous and culturally sophisticated. He preferred a woman who'd been married and had kids. "To me, that means they've been able to commit to someone else, and they know what kids require," he says. The other emotional qualities that matter, he says, are kindness, generosity, empathy, and an ability to be supportive during difficult times.

Gregory sometimes questions whether he is too "picky." He dismisses some profiles with a snap judgment. "I ask myself why I am doing that," he says. "Obviously, it hasn't worked. I haven't met the love of my life."

Could he compromise on any of his demands? He hesitates, then says that maybe he could forgo the outdoor activity as long as she still likes to travel.

Gregory knows he may be setting up roadblocks. "I've lived much of the last eighteen years on my own," he says. "I got used to solitude and am stuck in my ways. When I look at profiles, I wonder how much our histories will mesh."

The nature of online dating is partly to blame, he says. "It's like choosing from a big menu. It encourages some dysfunctional behavior. You might bypass someone who's wonderful."

Takeaways

What does this comparison between Dennis and Gregory tell us? It's simplistic to assume that, by itself, a short list of must-haves will immediately lead to relationship success. Yet having a short, realistic list does indicate you've figured out what's essential and you've ditched the rest. It also suggests you're open to different kinds of people, which improves your odds of finding love.

If you've got a long, detailed inventory of must-haves, ask yourself this: What's its *real* purpose? To find a good partner? Or to feed a fantasy?

Gregory knew there was something amiss in his search for "the love of my life." Several months after our first conversation, he was thrilled to tell me he was at the "beginning of a wonderful new relationship." He'd noticed her profile before but hadn't been "captivated" by it. So he hadn't reached out to her.

"I looked at her again and thought, *She really sounds nice*," he says.

He can't remember exactly why she didn't make the first cut (or the second or third), but he thinks the turnoff was her age. He's almost seventy and she's sixty-seven. He'd prefer someone at least ten years younger. When he met her, he realized that his stereotype about age didn't hold up. "She's fit and outdoorsy," he says.

A year later, he told me, "we've met each other's families." Things looked good. Two years after that, their relationship was thriving.

Gregory may have loosened his demands just enough. He may not have understood how he was undermining his mission, but he knew something had to change. Being willing to consider a woman closer to his age rather than holding out for a fantasy younger one may have led him to the love of his life.

Section II

Start Dating

Chapter Three

Master the Mechanics and Manners of Online Dating

You've done the headwork. You know who you are, what you need, what you can compromise on, and what you won't tolerate. You've taken the usual advice—for example, to join community or hobby groups where you might meet like-minded people. You've let your friends know you'd like to meet someone. All good things.

You probably need to do more. Often there aren't enough single age-appropriate partners in your friends network or community. More and more people are meeting on a dating site.

If you haven't used an online dating service, I'd like to acquaint you with how it works. It's helpful to understand how to use online dating to your best advantage. But keep in mind it's just a tool. You'll still need to figure out the essential qualities you need in a partner and how to navigate the emotional ups and downs of dating, however you do it.

Whether you're fifty, sixty, seventy, or eighty, online dating can be plodding, intoxicating, disheartening, hilarious, hurtful, and eye-opening. If you can (mostly) enjoy the journey, it can lead you to the love of your life.

Why Date Online?

I'm a big fan. Online, I find opportunities available nowhere else. When I was ready to date after Alan died, I told everyone I knew that I'd like to be fixed up. Most said they didn't know anybody. Yet when I went online, I found hundreds of men in my age group. Some lived in my neighborhood. Some I'd probably stood behind in the grocery checkout line. Some knew people I knew. Others lived farther away; I probably never would have met them except online.

That's the great thing about online dating. Those who are available announce it. You don't have to surreptitiously check out their ring finger at a café or ask leading questions to find out. Are there also people online you want to avoid? Absolutely, and I'll give you clues for spotting them.

Do you have fears about meeting people online? They're usually based on scary (usually untrue) stories you've heard. "A friend who's met some nice guys dared me to do eHarmony," says one divorced fifty-seven-year-old in the South. "In my world, that's like trying to meet a serial killer." She did try it, and she met her now-husband, who, by the way, is not a serial killer.

One sixty-eight-year-old woman in a mid-Atlantic city says, "I tried it before my divorce was final. It took courage I never knew I had." Because she was also afraid of ax murderers, she did a lot of research first, reading advice online and asking her girlfriends. You definitely want to educate yourself, not only to protect yourself from scam artists but to understand the realities and risks of dating online and to become alert to some common bad behaviors.

When things go wrong in a relationship formed online, some people blame the process. One divorcée in her late fifties found that a guy she'd been dating for months was super-possessive. Her conclusion? "This experience makes me question my judgment and meeting people randomly," she says. "With a fix-up, you can vet the guy." Maybe. But another just-divorced woman in her fifties was "ghosted" (an online term for someone who disappears without explanation) by someone introduced by friends.

This is my belief: Finding someone online is just a convenient method for meeting many different people. If, at the deepest level, you want to find someone who respects and loves you, you can find that person online. If, unfortunately, you gravitate to people who treat you badly, I guarantee you can find that person, too, whether online, at a bar, at your gym, or in your house of worship.

How to Pick a Dating Site and Set Up Your Profile

Decide Which Site Is Best for You

- Do you want the widest possible range of choices? Then start with a large site like Match.com, Plenty of Fish, or Zoosk.
- Would you like to choose prospects yourself or have the site match you? Most services offer both.
- Do you want to stay within your age range and race or another niche group? OurTime, Christian Mingle, JDate, Black-PeopleMeet, or AsianDating are some of those available.
- Do you want a free service or a paid one? Some people believe paying means you're more serious (or have more money). Others say it makes no difference. Many sites offer both. One warning, though: Even if the service is free, it will try to sell you additional services.
- Some websites attract a specific demographic—for example, city dwellers or suburbanites, highly educated people versus

less so. Get a free trial and search right away to find out how many people are in your preferred categories. If it's very few, cancel and move on (unless you see someone who seems perfect for you; after all, you only need one).

Choose Photos

When I look through profiles, I can't believe how many people are not smiling or even look sullen in their photos. Many photos are not in focus. Sometimes you can see a disembodied hand on a shoulder. No, no. Make an effort. Have a friend take shots and help you choose. It might be worthwhile to hire a professional. You need a good headshot, a whole-body view, and maybe one that shows you skiing, gardening, or baking bread, whatever you enjoy.

Write Your Profile

Who are you? What are you most proud of? What's quirky about you? Your profile should be both POSITIVE and SPECIFIC. Of course you have flaws like everyone else. Of course you've had hardships in life, maybe in love. But don't write about those things. If you're energetic and love to be out and about, *say* so, and say *what* you do, for example, theater, museums, hiking. If you like modern art, mention details: *Calder is my hero!* Like to garden? Proud of your juicy tomatoes? Your peonies? Say so. Love to cook? What's your favorite dish or cuisine?

Get help from friends on this. They'll be able to say what's special about you more easily than you can. And have them read and edit when you're done.

When you create an email address for contact, pick something specific and positive. I usually go with some play on "wordsmith," since I'm a writer. If you're looking for a serious relationship, avoid sexual come-ons like HotForYou or SexyLady or anything of that ilk. Better handles are: BestBaker, BraveLady, OutdoorsIsMe, JazzyPianist, QuickToLaugh.

How to Protect Yourself from Predators, Players, Bad Bets, and Eternal Pen Pals

You will hear this basic safety advice from many people. Before you know that you can trust someone:

- Do NOT give out identifying information: your full name, street address, home phone number, regular email address, or employer.
- Be sure your photos don't show your address, license plate, or any other identifying information.
- Always meet in public
- Never get in anyone's car

These precautions will safeguard you against con artists. Be aware and you'll be safe.

Learn to Spot Predators and Scammers

- Do not respond to anyone, especially from a foreign country (bad English is a clue) who tells you a heartbreaking story and sooner or later will ask for money.

- Do not respond to over-the-top flattery from someone who's never met you. Ignore people who say only "Hi, gorgeous," or "Hi, handsome." They've blanketed the Web with these and figure some gullible or desperate people will bite. Stop writing to anyone who claims to have fallen madly in love with you without ever meeting you. These people *want* something. Maybe money. Maybe sex with no strings.

- Avoid people who seem too good to be true. A woman from Vietnam who's thirty years younger than you and claims to adore you (without having met you). Maybe she wants a green card. A thirty-five-year-old man who looks movie-star handsome with muscles to die for claims to love women in their sixties. He may be a player. That photo may not even be real. To check whether it was lifted from another site, drag and drop the photo into Google Image search. Even if you can't locate the photo online, this person is almost certainly a predator of some kind. Do *not* be flattered.

Spot Bad Bets Right Away

A bad bet is anyone not ready for a relationship. If her profile bristles with things she *doesn't want* and everything *you must be*, she's at least unrealistic, probably angry. If he complains about his exes or the awful, dishonest, fat people he's met, steer clear.

If prospects tell you almost nothing about themselves or send you a generic email that shows they haven't even read your profile, that can signal desperation or lack of seriousness. If they boast about themselves but ask nothing about you, take that as a bad sign. Read their profile and emails carefully. A phone conversation can expand your impressions.

Don't Waste Time with a Pen Pal

A lot of lonely people online have intimate correspondences with people they never intend to meet. Some are articulate, sensitive, witty people with whom it is a joy to interact. If a pen pal is what you want, by all means correspond, but do not mistake this for a relationship.

If she lives far away and is unlikely to ever travel your way, stop writing.

If he lives nearby but avoids meeting after several emails, he probably doesn't really want to meet. Long correspondences encourage fantasies that can pop like a bubble the minute you lay eyes on each other.

My Own Tips and Tricks for Online Dating

Over many years, I've had hundreds of first dates, many second dates, several short-term relationships, and a couple of till-death-do-us-part unions. These are my strategies for success online.

I tried different websites: I met people on all of them, but I met most on Match.com because it has the biggest pool of people. That said, I've known people who have met the love of their life on JDate, eHarmony, Plenty of Fish, and OkCupid.

I got a photographer friend to take flattering photos of me: head shots and full-length shots. I picked ones where my smile was welcoming (not too broad, because then I thought my chin looked too pointy).

Since I'm a writer, I wrote a profile that was articulate and witty and appealed to the kind of smart man I hoped to find. If you're not good at this, get a friend to help you, or hire a ghostwriter. Most dating coaches offer this service (and you can find tons of them online).

There are a few things I'd like you to know as soon as your profile is up. Dating online takes work. Even after the start-up requirements, the process requires time, effort, and attention, especially at the beginning. It usually gets easier (and less breathlessly paced) after the first few months.

Most people receive a flurry of attention in the first weeks. Some daters have been registered for months or even years. After a while, people who've been at it for some time see the same profiles circle around. They may have met some or decided against meeting them. Then *you* show up. Fresh meat! Many pounce at once.

Use this initial time well, even if it's exhausting. Pay attention to each email and do not reject anyone reasonable out of hand. If you hear from some you consider maybes, write each a brief note, leaving open the possibility that you might be in touch later.

If one of the first people you meet strikes a chord, you might decide, if you're like me, to concentrate on him. (But never assume you're "exclusive" unless you ask and get a yes.) If someone else interesting writes, do respond. I usually wrote something like this: *Your profile is very appealing, and if I'd read it two weeks ago, I certainly would have wanted to talk. But I've just started to date someone, and I prefer to date one person at a time. If I find myself free again, may I contact you?* Everyone to whom I sent such a note said yes. And sometimes we did get to meet if the current relationship didn't work out.

I didn't wait to be "matched" by the website. I went to the "advanced search" option and looked myself. I didn't care about religion or money, but I did care about education and marital status. I wrote to many people with whom I felt kinship. I knew that some profiles were still up even though these guys were actually no longer available or interested, so I'd check the last time they were "active" on the site (possibly only window-shopping while dating someone exclusively).

When I wrote, I always referred to something in his profile. If someone with real potential didn't reply, I tried again. I felt no shame. I got many responses and many dates. Sometimes I got a reply to my second note: It might explain that he was dating someone now but might get back to me. Or he might say he hadn't noticed my first email because he got so many, but let's talk.

After two or three emails, I always suggested we talk on the phone. I used my cell phone number, which wasn't listed anywhere. Sometimes I was turned off by the conversation. If that happened, I thanked him and said I could tell that the chemistry wasn't right, and I'd learned to trust my gut. If he seemed a little nervous, I gave him the benefit of the doubt and arranged a coffee date.

After I'd been on a site for a while and emails stopped pouring in, I searched out profiles marked "new," and if Mr. New looked interesting, I contacted him immediately. One man I dated for almost a year told me he'd been on a site for "five minutes" when I "pounced," and he hardly got to meet any other women. He really liked me, so he soon stopped grousing and forgot about meeting other women.

For first dates, I usually suggested meeting at a relatively quiet Italian café in my neighborhood. My friends told me my hair and lipstick didn't have to be perfect, but *I* felt better when I'd just looked in the mirror and remembered my dad saying, *Cute as a button*. I'd try to be early so I could make last-minute fixes. Or I'd stop at a bathroom down the block so I could make a grand entrance, feeling confident. Either way, I greeted my date with a dazzling smile, however he looked.

I found some dates appealing but could tell the feeling wasn't mutual, starting with hello. I once had a date with a very tall, good-looking man whose profile said he wanted to be with a woman five-nine or taller, although on the phone he insisted that all he really cared about was being with a smart woman who could talk about literature and the arts. At first sight, he looked down at four-eleven me from his lofty height and said, "Wow, you really are short." That was it. Still, he took me out to an elegant dinner and made an effort to be courteous and entertaining. I've had coffee with men who never made eye contact. They looked everywhere but at me as we talked.

Some men who'd been online awhile asked me about my dating experiences there. Generally, that meant they weren't turned on by me but were making pleasant conversation and maybe learning something. Sometimes I would have been glad for a second date, but I could tell (usually) by the way we parted that it wasn't going to happen. Other times I expected a call, and *that* didn't happen. I'd like to tell you I never took this personally. Not quite true.

Once I had a lovely date with a widower, a long, engaging conversation over coffee, extended with a walk in the park at his suggestion. But he never called. I may have written him a note saying I had a good time; sometimes I did if I wanted to encourage another date. About a year later, this widower called. I reminded him that we'd met, and he said yes, we had. "And *now* you're calling me?" I said, clearly hostile. "Well, if you feel that way," he said, "let's say goodbye."

I never got to find out why he hadn't called after our first date. I never got to try again with this man I'd liked. How stupid was that? Luckily, I was more smart than stupid. You can be smart, too.

Acquaint Yourself with Online Customs: Be Prepared for These Common Bad Behaviors

There are many lovely, courteous people on your dating website, but even they can't reply to every note. If someone ignores you or drops out of contact, the disappointment may sting. But if you know the behavior is common, you can brush it off more easily. Remember, these bad manners have names because they're so prevalent online. Life coach Treva Brandon Scharf's blog post, "The 3 Dirtiest Words in Dating," offers a useful read on this subject.

Ghosting

After several emails or dates, he disappears without explanation and does not answer texts or calls.

Backburning

She's available only on Mondays or Thursdays. Assuming she's not married (and you have to determine that), she's probably dating other people. She'd like to keep you on the line in case things don't work out with others.

Benching

Guys like this want to keep you around but aren't serious about moving forward. They send out mixed signals, with the occasional flirtatious message to keep you answering.

Breadcrumbing

She sends you come-hither notes to keep you involved and hoping, but she doesn't plan to meet you. Cut off correspondence that doesn't quickly lead to a meeting, and you'll avoid this.

Most Effective Communication Strategies

If you wait for daters to contact you, you'll probably have some dates. If you search out and contact prospects, you'll have more. Whether you're a man or a woman is irrelevant. "It's not like when we learned how to date, where a girl had to sit by the phone waiting for the boy to call her," one now-partnered woman in her sixties told me. She wrote to those *she* found interesting. Some responded; some didn't. But one of those who did reply became her long-term partner.

She dated online in the most effective way. As (now former) eHarmony CEO Grant Langston says, "The single least productive behavior is passivity. The most productive is reaching out and saying hello to as many people as you possibly can. Are they writing back? Are they interested? It doesn't matter. You want to create as much activity as you possibly can. The people who matter will respond, and the rest don't matter one bit."

That was certainly my strategy. All my life, my friends marveled at what they called my chutzpah, my nerve. One said of me long ago, "Francine learned that if she asks for what she wants, she's likelier to get it than if she doesn't." I don't hold myself up as a model in all things relationship, but asking loses you nothing and often gets you the thing you want most. One divorced new dater wrote to a fifty-five-year-old guy online who listed himself as Catholic and specified his age range for a partner as forty-six to fifty-five. "Would you consider dating a fifty-eight-year-old Jewish woman?" she asked. "Yes," he wrote, noticing her profile for the first time. They've now been together over fifteen years.

Chapter Four

Reconsider Your Automatic Categories

Many daters tell me they're stuck. The older you are, they say, the harder it is to find the right someone with the right chemistry who also meets your other requirements: location, religion, parenting status, income and education level, politics, and the rest. Forming an intimate relationship without these requirements might mean tolerating differences or making major lifestyle changes.

Usually, at your age, the only person you have to please is yourself. Gone is the demand to select someone "appropriate" for your parents and your circle, someone of your own ethnic group, race, religion, or class. Gone is the need to find someone who will make a good parent for the children you hope to have. How much ambition and earning power or money your partner has is—or could be—irrelevant to your current time of life. Still, many people automatically stick to the old categories, stereotypes, and myths that severely (and unnecessarily) limit their choices. To expand your possibilities for the emotionally rewarding bond you crave, try rethinking these reflexive limits.

Online, you've probably checked off your basic demographic boxes. Maybe you have sound reasons for ruling out whole groups. Or maybe you're just operating on autopilot.

Take politics. In our fractured nation many of us feel that anyone on the opposite side of a political divide must be a horrible person with disgusting values. Yet chemistry does not always ignite along political, religious, or ethnic lines. People who've dated for a while without finding anyone may have fished in too small a pool. Reconsider your limits. Depending on who you are, your partner's beliefs may be profoundly important. Or they may be an issue you can work around.

Paul,* seventy-six, and Virginia,* seventy-nine, both residents of the Great Plains region, came together despite lifestyle and political differences. She is a devout churchgoer and observes strict standards of behavior and language. From a life wrangling horses, he says, "I have a filthy mouth." Still, he understands, as he says, "She is very sensitive to 'God damn,' so I try to avoid that." When he lapses and lets loose his colorful vocabulary, she comes down on him hard. Politically, she describes herself as "very conservative" with "strong opinions." He is decidedly liberal and an MSNBC junkie.

Their story is illuminating because they didn't have shopping lists or even know they wanted a partner. First they were friends. When romantic feelings developed, they could weigh their differences against *knowing* each other. They didn't have to decide in the *abstract* whether the other's leanings were worth accommodating. They'd each experienced the other as someone who could support them through a crisis.

For years, they'd socialized as couples with their late spouses at the southern resort where they'd spent winters. They'd liked each other without feeling any special attraction. When their spouses were slowly dying at the same nursing home, they bonded. "We were propping each other up, crying on the phone," Paul says. "We leaned on each other, but not in a romantic way."

After their spouses died, Paul and Virginia continued talking long-distance and shared their loneliness. He began to think about her romantically, and she reciprocated. For an intimate relationship to work (and it has), they had to live with some big differences.

The subject of politics is challenging. "He's so terribly liberal," she says. "But he watches TV when I'm not there, or he wears headphones so I can't hear it. We choose not to discuss it. A couple of times, he riled my feathers. I had to have my word. And then it was over."

"She'll be eighty soon," he says. "As long as we don't deal with it, we're okay. At our age, we don't need *resolution* on these issues. We're not raising kids together."

None of their differences affect how much they laugh together or take comfort in loving each other. "We can't wait each night and each morning to snuggle together," she says. "He hugs with his whole body, and that's awesome."

If Paul and Virginia had been seeking a partner online, they probably would have ruled the other out because of differences. What they would have—ignorantly—been giving up! Is this you? Try to view each person as an individual and judge the whole person.

Weigh Your Demographic Preferences
Against More Intimate Needs

Imagine this. You've spotted an appealing profile that made you think this man or woman *could* be someone:

- who supports and loves you through a trauma with your kids or the death of a parent
- who cuddles with you morning and night and whenever you need affection
- who encourages you to be your best self and reminds you how great you are when you feel down
- who makes tender, passionate love to you
- who wants to hear about your day
- who does most of what you want without your having to ask
- will leave you alone when you need solitude
- can take care of himself and not expect you to fill all his needs
- will not mind when you take two weeks to see grandkids or go trekking in Nepal

Imagine someone who does all this BUT:

- doesn't share your religion or race
- doesn't have as much money as you do
- is not as tall or toned or attractive as you'd like
- lives two hours away or farther
- is older or younger than you prefer
- is less educated or cultured than you

Now, carefully weigh each of your long-held demands against the relationship you might have. What's most essential?

How Important Is Race to You?

For many people, race is a harder dividing line than religion or politics, but if you're willing to cross it, you widen your field. London psychotherapist Russell Thackeray tells of a female friend, white, who insisted on ten qualities that a partner absolutely *had* to have. Still hurt by a cheating spouse, she named her top three priorities as integrity, trustworthiness, and truthfulness. Oh, and he had to be sexually adventurous, exclusively with her.

Thackeray marvels that she found someone with all ten. He was Chinese. "They had a cultural problem at first, but fifteen years later, they're still together," Thackeray reports. "And although when they met, he was not sexually adventurous, he was open to it."

Rita,* seventy, a white college professor in New York, wanted a partner after her divorce. She checked "no preference" on race and other categories. "It didn't matter," she explains. "This was not someone I'd share decades of my life with, have kids with, all that stuff. I just needed someone to go to the movies with, talk with, sleep with, and with whom I could have companionship. I did, though, want us to have common interests."

She soon met George,* an African American man a few years younger who'd dropped out of college. He was smart and, like her, interested in the arts. She found him physically attractive. Nine years later, she and George are what sociologists term "living apart together" (LAT). They see each other often, talk every day, and share a great deal of their lives, but not everything.

"Age makes it easier to be with someone of another race," she says. "That whole family formation thing is not salient. You don't have to ask, 'Can I be a good parent to an African American child?'" As for their families, she notes that he has no children and her grown daughter was accepting of diverse couples, and she says, "All our parents are dead. We don't have to keep anyone happy besides ourselves."

He's shared with her what it's like to be black, she says, and that's really widened her worldview. Of their almost-decade-long relationship, she says, "The gears fit together pretty well. I'm content."

Must Your Partner Match You in Education or Cultural Background?

You have nothing to lose by trying a date with someone of a different background. After her husband left her, one sixty-eight-year-old professional woman did. When she joined a local social group, she met and dated several "blue-collar" guys. "They were as much fun as educated people," she says. Some of them were like her father. "He had to drop out of school but really made something of himself." She loved dating a multi-tattooed former marine, clinging to his strong back as they roared along on his Harley-Davidson. "He had a kind heart, and I had fun," she says. "He's still a friend."

Nancy,* a financial professional in her sixties, is in love with a man she'd have thought culturally inappropriate when she was younger. "I would not have accepted his religiosity or his lower-class origins: He's a rube from Arkansas," she says with affection. Now that doesn't matter at all.

What's most important is his thoughtfulness. Other things can be learned. From him, she's learned to be less snobbish and to value intrinsic qualities above surface sophistication. She's also found out that fishing can be fun with the right person. "And I have exposed him to things that make my life rich: arts, music, theater, dance," she says. "He's a willing learner."

Question Your Assumptions About Age —
Your Own and Other People's

In our youth-obsessed society, misconceptions about age are rampant. Studies show that most of us think of ourselves as looking, acting, even *feeling* ten years younger than we are. I can't tell you how many times I've heard the claim: "I look much younger than my age." Both men and women post twenty-year-old photos and believe they still look like that. One recently divorced woman of fifty told me she thought: *These guys are so* old. Then she realized she was the same age, and she began to see them differently.

Online, I routinely lopped off four years. I wanted to be seen as in my forties rather than fifty-two, then as in my fifties, not sixty-one. Now, I really *did* look younger. So I thought, anyway. "You look your age," a friend said. "You just look good for your age."

In person, I always told the truth. Most men expected and excused this lie. The older I (and my dates) got, the more I found that men lied, too.

Women pretend partly to combat the outmoded convention that men should be with younger women. This custom originated over thousands of years during which men valued women for their fertility. Recently, marriages have become more equal. "If he is the sort of man that makes you feel you ought to lie about your age, maybe he is *not* the sort of man you want for an egalitarian life partner," says historian Stephanie Coontz, author of *Marriage, a History: How Love Conquered Marriage*.

Many think that younger equals more attractive, fit, and healthy. Actually, after fifty, numerical age matters less than how a person ages. *That* depends on health, lifestyle, attitude, and genes.

When you set your target age range, consider the relative advantages and disadvantages of a large age gap. For example, Luke,* sixty and twice divorced, recently married a woman much closer to his own age than his previous spouses. She's able to understand the importance of family and the tragedy he endured of losing a son to cancer. "You're in the last stretch of your life," he says. "You get little ailments, and you're more aware of time." In the past, he was attracted to very young, beautiful women. "After a few years, it became apparent that the age gap was not appropriate," he says. "I'd say, *Remember when*, and then I'd say, *Oh, right, you weren't even born then.* You can't share a lot."

"The closer in age you are," says Houston therapist Mary Jo Rapini, "the more intimacy potential you have. Both partners are self-aware and want someone they can share life with on their level." That includes a shared historical vocabulary, she adds: "Our memories of youth grow stronger with age."

Jim Le Gette, eighty-one, for example, who was a child during World War II, married Carolyn Miller Parr, also eighty-one. "We were both eating macaroni-and-cheese casseroles because of the war," he says. "We shared that and similar experiences."

With larger age differences, the older one's energy can dwindle faster, disappointing a young partner still eager to spend weekends museum-hopping or hiking. Many age-matched couples speak of the comfort with each other's bodies, their limitations and changes with age. "I never feel self-conscious," one wife told me. "He knows what a sixty-year-old body looks like, and so do I."

Many have taken turns caring for the other through hip replacements, heart surgery, and shingles. Trading roles feels fair and right.

Maureen* and Larry,* who married at fifty-nine and fifty-four, respectively, are now seventy-four and sixty-nine. Last winter while ice-skating with their grandchildren, he fell and broke two ribs. "It was eye-opening for both of us," she says. "He'd never felt so helpless. I was his caregiver. But I've had more health issues than he has."

How Far Will You Go for Love? Cross a Bridge? Drive an Hour?

Most people have automatic cutoffs. In Manhattan, crossing a bridge makes some prospects "geographically undesirable." One widower agreed to make an exception and meet me; usually, he dated people only *in* Brooklyn. In St. Louis, bordered by the Mississippi and Missouri rivers, some folks won't "cross the river" (the Missouri) into St. Charles County; it's *across the river*. Yes, and it's a thirty-minute drive in either direction!

St. Louis therapist Patt Hollinger Pickett, author of *The Marriage Whisperer*, and her husband, now married eighteen years, still laugh at how they almost never met. He lived in suburban St. Charles; she lived in the city. When he read her profile, he passed. When she contacted him, he reconsidered and agreed to meet her. "On our first date," she recalls, "we talked and laughed a lot at dinner, then he walked me to my car and planted a big kiss on my lips. I was shocked but thought, *Okay, this tells me he's interested.*"

Others traveled much farther. They all say their relationship was worth it.

How Lorraine Came to Value Her Relationship over Staying Put

Lorraine* had no idea what a meaningful relationship could give her. She'd had a brief disastrous marriage to a man who was a compulsive gambler. Counseling did nothing. One day a burly guy showed up at her door. He handed her a card, saying, "This is where you take your son after we've cut off his finger."

Lorraine packed her tots into her car and drove off. With her parents' help, she got a job and built a career. "I was so unhappy I decided I would never marry again," she says. For years, parenting, career, and survival dominated her life. When she did start to date, she avoided any permanent relationship. "I just wanted to get out, do things, have fun with men," she says.

Her demands? A man who wanted no commitment but would respect her independence and financial stability. He also had to have good family values. Over forty years, she had several relationships, but no one became central to her life. "I had all-consuming, interesting jobs, lots of friends, and was comfortable enough financially to travel or do the things I liked," she says. "I never felt *less* being single."

She was sixty-three when she "stumbled on" Herb,* a recent widower, at a friend's wedding. They enjoyed talking. He gave her his number and suggested she call if she ever got up his way. He lived near San Francisco. Her life was rooted in Los Angeles, near her family and friends. She dismissed their meeting from her mind. But Herb called several times, and when business took her "his way," she let him know.

Herb planned an exciting twelve-hour day. They connected on many levels. She admired his commitment to his three grown sons; he traveled long distances to stay involved with them. He was smart and spoke knowledgeably about many subjects. "This was seductive to me emotionally and intellectually," she says. As they began taking turns commuting to spend weekends together, she felt scared. "I didn't like marriage, and I didn't want to live with anyone," she says.

They commuted for seven years. She enjoyed him but didn't realize she *loved* him. Until he broke it off. He'd reconnected with a high school friend, he told her, and she was moving in with him.

"I was devastated," Lorraine says. Her pain told her how deeply she loved him, how he added to her life in a way no one ever had. She grieved the loss.

A year later, Herb called, contrite. His new relationship had gone bust after three months. During it, he'd fallen into a deep depression.

That impulsive behavior, starting to live with a woman he'd known only slightly in school and only recently reconnected with, was totally out of character, he said, and he was deeply ashamed. (He would later realize in therapy that he'd acted out of suppressed grief for his wife.) He begged Lorraine to take him back.

After careful thought, she agreed to try it. "We realized that if this were to work, we'd have to live together," she says. It was a tough decision, but their relationship grew. They spend almost every night together except certain holidays.

Usually, they spend two weeks in her home, two in his. Whenever this changeover irritates her, she says, "In the past, I didn't want to compromise. Now I do, and it's okay. This is the first time I've been so deeply invested in a relationship. I truly love him. He makes me laugh all day long, and I feel loved. He's there for me through illness and injuries. He cancels everything else. I come first."

Lorraine, perhaps like you, faced many obstacles to a relationship. Is moving from city to city every two weeks a major pain? Of course. Is it worth it? To her, absolutely. Also to others I've met who've rearranged their lives in ways they once could never have imagined.

What if Someone Can't Afford My Lifestyle?

Another must for many is a partner with similar financial resources. If *you* can find this and have chemistry, go for it. But if not, think about money from a new angle.

People want someone financially stable. Of course. Who wants a partner who spends money she doesn't have, piles up debt, gambles regularly, and spends thoughtlessly? Women worry that a man with little money will want to live off them. Men suspect that women without money are looking for a "sugar daddy." But what about the many over-fifties who live modestly within limited means? The world is filled with people who had their bank accounts and retirement funds drained by divorce or were laid off from a job due to corporate downsizing. Some have retired on a small pension or rely entirely on Social Security. Others had a business bankrupted by the Great Recession or the pandemic. Some opted for a meaningful career in the arts that never made them a high earner. Are they all out of the question?

Yes, you say. I want someone who can afford the restaurants I go to, Broadway shows, seasons at the beach. I want someone who can pay her own medical bills. Many insisting on this have searched fruitlessly for years. So I say: Think more flexibly.

Celia* did. It was an uncomfortable stretch at first. A widow of sixty-eight who was well off, she had the typical worries about an impecunious boyfriend. Would he end up living off her? Would they never vacation together?

She hesitated to meet Hugh.* His profile displayed excellent writing and wit. He was clearly smart and cultured. He had a brilliant smile, a handsome face topped by a luxuriant head of silver hair. He listed his income range on the low end. *What the hell*, she recalls thinking, *it's only coffee*.

When they met, they lit each other up. "In person, that smile was dazzling," she says.

Hugh, seventy-two, had been a modestly successful entrepreneur until 2008, when his business tanked. He was subsisting almost entirely on Social Security and a small pension. *Poor*, she thought.

But she kept seeing him. They had so much fun, lobbing wordplay back and forth across the table. And they laughed a lot. "He could talk about his feelings," she says. "And when I shared my grief over my husband's loss, his eyes teared up. This was a man I might love."

Over the course of several dates, movies and dinners out, they always split the check. As they grew closer, she learned more about his financial situation. He really was poor. He could afford his tiny rent-controlled apartment and not much else.

Over time, his financial situation mattered less. They spent many nights together, always at her place. Sex, she says, was "amazing." He was not only a thoughtful and caring lover; he was an all-around good guy. At her apartment, he automatically took care of whatever needed doing, from buying lightbulbs to chopping broccoli. When they went out, he was scrupulous about paying his half. "He treated me for my birthday," she says, "but I made sure I picked a cheapish place. I didn't miss going to some trendy joint."

Now, three years later, he virtually lives with her while keeping his own apartment. She's fine with paying the bills for her place. They split groceries and movies in half. Recently, she's begun to treat them to season-theater subscriptions. "We used to negotiate what shows he wanted to see enough to cough up a hundred bucks," she says. "Then I thought, *You know what, I'm happy to have someone to go with, I can afford it, and why not?* Sometimes he surprises me with a bouquet of flowers. I love him. I'm happy."

The income difference for Brenda* and Jerry* is less dramatic. At least she thinks so. She actually has no idea how much he has. "We never talk about money," she says. When the two widowed people started dating twenty years ago, they talked briefly about who would pay for what. "He wanted to pay for dinners," she says. "I began buying the big-ticket items like the season at the Hollywood Bowl."

Fifteen years later, when he suggested moving in with her because his rent was going up, she agreed. Some months he gives her money for expenses. Some months he doesn't. "It doesn't bother me," she says. "I know I have more money, and I know he's bothered that he doesn't have as much as he'd hoped he would for retirement. We're happy together. We don't keep score."

How Rethinking a "Prefer Not" and an
"Absolutely Not" Led to Long-Term Happiness

If you recall, Richard had ping-ponged from stable but boring partners to exciting but troubled women. In his late fifties, he met Anna,
who seemed ideal: She had character and personality, stability and
excitement. But she didn't fit two important boxes he'd checked: parenting status and religion.

He didn't want someone with kids still at home; Anna's teenage
daughter lived with her. Even more troubling, he'd believed, was her
devout Christianity. "As a secular humanist Jew, I could not accept
any whose religious beliefs would be considered truth for everyone," he says. He worried about being with anyone who thought that
everyone outside of *her* faith was excluded from grace, an infidel or
the equivalent in that religion.

He struggled internally with the parenting issue. His own children were in their thirties. He'd never envisioned parenting again.
Can I deal with this? he asked himself. He met Anna's daughter and
found she was quite independent. Richard factored in that her biological father was present in her life, so he would not have to be a
father figure. Then this educator, whose work involved advising parents, asked himself: *Why can't I deal with a fifteen-year-old girl?*

Anna's religious beliefs were harder. But Anna was so exception-
ally the kind of woman he'd been searching for! So he worked to find
a way forward with her.

Anna was also conflicted. So many things about Richard were
right. But as a devout Christian, she'd been taught that marrying
"out" was to be "unfaithful to my faith," she says. They talked repeatedly about what faith meant to them and what they could accept. As
part of the process, they wrote down what each needed to make the
relationship possible.

Richard calls what he wrote his "platform": Anna was to recognize that he was secure in his belief system and that she was not to proselytize. For his part, he would respect her attending church on her own, and would participate in nonreligious social events at church. If things worked out and she wanted a religious marriage ceremony, that was okay with him.

Anna had begun dating looking for a Christian, but she now asked herself, what did that mean? Her ex-husband was a Christian, but his fundamentalism was rigid and more focused on sin than on helping the unfortunate or leading an ethical life, things she valued more.

She struggled to decide. "I realized that Richard's values and ethics are in line with mine," she says. "I could still have those values without the religion." Nearly twenty years later, she says, "What I value in Richard, among so many other things, is his integrity and how he values our relationship, which he values as his first priority. Being in love and having such a good fit has been a revelation."

Richard learned what others have learned: It's hard to decide what's acceptable in the abstract. Only within the context of an otherwise highly desirable relationship can you weigh a negative trait or situation.

I can't stress this enough: Think carefully about what's important to you and then decide what's *essential*. If you find that rare emotional and physical chemistry you're seeking, you may be able to let go of things you believed were nonnegotiable.

Chapter Five

Date as a Realist: Are Negative Attitudes or Fantasies Sabotaging You?

I f you want love, examine your attitudes and beliefs about dating. Feeling pessimistic? No good! You're bound to undermine yourself. On the other hand, does each email set off a frenzy of expectation? Disappointment will follow.

The best attitudes to adopt are these: be hopeful, be confident, be realistic, be open. Think of the late, great comedian Robin Williams slapping the side of his head and exclaiming: "Reality! What a concept!"

Staying in reality is not as easy to do as to say. You may not realize that finding the right partner takes *work* and *time*. The average stay on eHarmony, says (former) CEO Grant Langston, is a year. Some people take much longer, dating on and off, trying different sites, having brief relationships, taking breaks, and then going back online. Along the way, these daters get better at choosing and meeting.

Adjust your expectations. If you get frustrated after a few months, believing *I should have met someone by now*, remind yourself that most people do not find love so quickly. But those who keep at it eventually do. Becoming discouraged quickly is why many people fail.

Troubleshooting: Having No Luck at Dating?

If no one is writing or replying, revise your online presence. Get help rewriting your bio and posting new photos. Having many first dates that don't go anywhere is typical. But if *nobody* you meet wants to see you again, take a hard look at what you're projecting on dates. Do you dominate the conversation and express no interest in your date? Do you express contempt and anger when you talk about your ex?

Try to become conscious of the emotional signals you're sending out. If you project negativity, attack your attitudes at the source: Look within. What do you see? Anger? Cynicism? Desperation?

Ask your friends. What do they hear when you talk about dating? Do you convey hostility or suspicion? Are you harshly judgmental? If you can't identify what you're radiating—a hard thing for any of us to see about ourselves—you may want to consult a therapist or a dating coach.

Therapist Karen Osterle recalls an eighty-year-old widower, Sid,* who wanted to find someone. He was charming and erudite but also prickly. He didn't know how to connect with others. He was out of touch with his own feelings. Unknowingly, he was fending people off. "I showed him what he's emanating," Osterle says.

Therapists typically demonstrate the emotional vibes you're giving off by unmasking them during your sessions. Osterle found Sid oppositional. He resisted whatever she said or withdrew to some private space. She spoke frankly to him. "I'm feeling irritated with you right now," she would say. "Are you also annoyed with me?"

Over many such interactions, she helped the struggling Sid unearth what he was feeling at any moment. He learned to notice changes in his physical sensations and to link them to emotions he didn't realize he was feeling. Anger, for example, he came to identify by a surge of adrenaline and his hands clawing the air as he talked. Tension at the back of his neck signaled anxiety.

"There's a way you erect this wall of negativity, and you're behind it," Osterle once told him. "You're detached from me and probably from other people."

With her coaching, he was ready to connect with others.

If you tell yourself, *I've had no success*, reframe what success looks like. Have you met several fairly nice people within a few months? That's *success!* You're doing something right. What's wrong is concluding that because you haven't met "the one," then dating isn't working for you.

Carol,* a fifty-eight-year-old long-divorced woman had not dated in thirty years when she went online. Although she had more than ten coffee dates in her first months on Match.com, she declared she was "fed up" and ready to "give up." Then she heard back from Ken.*

Ken was a computer programmer about her age whom she'd written to a month earlier. He looked warm and friendly in his photo. He said that he, too, listened to NPR. They'd read many of the same books. They were instantly attracted when they met. Over several dates, they talked and talked. They didn't want their dates to end.

Carol and Ken are now living together. When they met, she was about to pack it in. On their second date, she told him her favorite four-letter word had become "next!" He prophesied correctly: "I'm gonna change your favorite four-letter word to 'more'!"

If Carol had given up, she never would have met Ken. Maybe not anyone.

The story of MaryJane,* a sixty-seven-year-old divorced woman, is more how online dating typically goes. Her journey occurred over seven years. "I would try online for three months," she says, "then I'd go off for six and try another site. I was online and off from 2011 to 2018." She had several brief relationships and became a savvier dater. She understood that dating was a *process*, and she lived her life as she did it. In 2018 she met her husband. The key to success? Not rushing dating, taking breaks, and not giving up.

Beware of Negative Attitudes and Myths: Yours

Some people sign up for a dating site already disgruntled. *Why should I have to do this? Why can't I meet someone in a more organic way?* Some begin dating online as a last resort, almost certain to fail. They believe self-defeating myths like some I've mentioned and others:

- *No one will date someone my age.*
- *If you're not thin and attractive, no one will date you.*
- *They're all narcissists and cheaters, like my ex.*
- *All the good ones are married.*
- *No one will want me.*

These pessimistic beliefs are self-fulfilling prophecies. "If you believe that being in your fifties means that you are 'old,' then your confirmation bias—the tendency to interpret new evidence as confirmation of one's preexisting belief—will kick in to make this come true," says therapist Russell Thackeray. "If you believe your chances for happiness are diminished and that no one else could possibly enrich your life, you will move toward all your single and miserable friends (after all, misery loves company)."

Your attitude will also color how you *perceive* people online. If you see everyone through a cloud, you'll squander opportunities.

Candace,* for example, a fifty-five-year-old divorced woman in Manhattan, was stuck between the pros and cons of a man who'd emailed her. He looked okay and seemed like a maybe. But he didn't act like the others. He insisted on a phone call before meeting, and he also insisted on having dinner rather than coffee. She found this annoying. She wanted a quick meet and a thumbs-up or thumbs-down. Yet she agreed to a phone call and then to dinner.

When the night approached, she almost canceled. "He had three strikes against him," she says. "Strike one: He had a terrible New York accent. Strike two: He was in insurance—boring! Strike three: His kids didn't go to fancy schools. I grew up on the Upper East Side, where it was all about where you went to school and how you dress and how much money you have."

At the last minute, she says, "I thought, *Fuck it. I'm just gonna go.*" When she saw him, he was "cuter than in his photo." Even more seductive, he'd read and remembered her profile. She'd written, *I'm a confirmed chocoholic and don't plan to change.* As he stood up to greet her, she spotted a package of deluxe chocolates in his hand. "From then on, he was a yes," she says.

He also was smarter, more interesting, and more athletic than she'd assumed. Funny, too. "He makes me smile," she says. Two years later, they're together, and she finds his accent endearing.

The important thing about this example isn't that her decision led to a great relationship. The date easily could have been a washout. But if she'd decided to cancel, she'd have had no date and no *opportunity*.

Hold Your Negative Beliefs Up to Reality

Millions of people over fifty are finding new partners. Why shouldn't you? What are *your* self-defeating beliefs? To combat them, examine the evidence for and against each one.

No one will date someone over fifty.

Negative voice: People say so. I'm over fifty, and I don't get asked out. My single friends don't date, either.

Reality: Look around you. You probably know people who are dating. You've heard about lots of others. Read the scores of articles about the boom in online dating. Lots of people in their fifties, sixties, seventies, and eighties have found new partners. This demographic wave is huge. Why shouldn't you be part of it?

If you don't get asked out, maybe that's because you haven't put yourself where there are single people your age. Even more important, you feel and project negativity.

No one will be interested in you if you can't have sex.

Negative voice: People say so. I think so. Viagra commercials make it seem that you can't be desirable without an erection. I don't see a lot of movies where old people have sex. Everyone wants sex, and I can't perform anymore.

Reality: Everyone is different. Some people in their sixties and seventies want as much sex as they can get. Others are done and just want to hold hands and snuggle. And you probably haven't seen the right movies. Check out *Something's Gotta Give* and *Book Club* (with stars Diane Keaton, Jane Fonda, Candice Bergen, and Mary Steenburgen) or a series like *Grace and Frankie.*

If you're not thin and attractive, no one will date you.

Negative voice: I don't feel attractive because I'm twenty pounds overweight. I wouldn't date someone who's fat.

Reality: Yes, there's discrimination against fat people in our society. But look at the older people you've seen who've met someone. Are they all thin and gorgeous? They most certainly are not. Maybe the partner you meet will also be overweight or bald or have wrinkles and paunches. Older people can look attractive, but they do *not* look like young people. Also, many mature men and women have told me that appearance is less important to them now than other qualities. Based on her personal experience and what she's seen as a dating coach, Sandy Weiner says, "A grown-up mature man is looking for a woman his age. He doesn't care about a few extra pounds. He loves her feistiness, her opinions, and the rich life she's lived."

They're all narcissists and cheaters, like my ex.

Negative voice: In my previous relationships, every partner turned out to be a narcissist or a cheater.

Reality: Millions of people are meeting and finding love every day. It flies in the face of reason that they are all a certain kind of messed-up person. It is possible to find a partner who is none of these bad things, but first you will have to discover what it is in *you* that draws you to a certain type. Carefully read the section in Chapter Seven: Make Sure You Haven't Chosen the Same Bad-for-You Mate.

No one will want me.

Negative voice: My previous relationships haven't worked out. I don't feel lovable. Why would anyone want me?

Reality: The belief that you are not lovable comes from inside, not outside. You probably need to do more headwork.

If, despite overwhelming evidence to the contrary, you can't let go of this belief, do these CBT exercises. Identify your negative attitudes. Every time one pops into your head, replace it with a realistic positive. For example, if you think, *No one will date someone over fifty*, marshal all the support you've gathered and talk back to that negative voice. Do it as often as you need to.

As author Seth J. Gillihan, a licensed psychologist who specializes in CBT, explains, just thinking, *I'll never find anyone* leads to discouragement, even hopelessness. Then you don't try as hard or you sabotage dates. But if you catch these thoughts as they occur and then counter them, your attitudes will change, and so will your behavior—for the good.

Listen to the voices in this book. Develop a hopeful attitude, and project energy and optimism. These will look great on you.

If you start by believing, as Kira* did, *All the good ones are taken*, you'll automatically assume anyone not "taken" is no good.

Kira, a beautiful, successful never-married woman, waged a battle with her negative assumptions when she dated online in her fifties. She was determined to find both the love and marriage that had eluded her. "The pool was shrinking," she says. "All the good ones were taken."

How did she know this? "I wasn't meeting them," she says.

Believing they weren't out there, she failed to see any good ones for almost two years. How she defined "good" was a barrier. She had done a significant amount of headwork: a whole self-help bazaar of books, videos, and workshops. She had modified her definition of a good partner. In her forties, her top priorities had been "strikingly handsome" and "a high earner." "Now I made attractiveness and income less important than substance. I wanted someone with education, a sense of humor, who was easy to talk to, kind, confident, and athletic."

Despite believing the odds were against her, she forced herself to go on dates. She knew she had to meet people to have any chance at all. "You have to go out there and meet them," she says. "There are a lot of whiny women just sitting at home. I say, 'Just shut up and do it!' To some extent, it's a numbers game." The process, she says, was "agony." "While at first it can be fun, it can become very depressing. Staying motivated was a challenge."

The guy's photo still mattered. "You want to be attracted when looking at photos," she says. But when she realized that photos don't always reveal a person's appeal, she had a breakthrough. Her new husband didn't seem that "cute" in his picture, but his profile shone. "He was funny, he was cool, and he *got* it," she says. "He wasn't a weirdo or a dork." She says now that you have to be "forgiving" about photos. "Lots of men don't know much about posting a great picture, and they're often embarrassed to ask for help."

At fifty-seven, she finally won her battle with self-sabotaging beliefs. Sadly, there are men and women still subverting their search for love. One divorced woman in her seventies told me that of all the men out there, if they were smart, they weren't attractive. If they were attractive, they weren't smart. There was no one who was both. Certainly, there was no one *she* could see.

Dial Down the Fantasy

As I've said before, stomp out those negative expectations. But beware of fantasy, too.

Kira, like many pessimist daters, also suffered from overblown hopes. These distort reality in the opposite direction. Again and again, she'd identify a man as "the one"—on *paper*. Before meeting, she imagined romantic scenarios. Yet when she met her dream prospects, she felt nothing and left feeling crushed.

She realized that "spending too much time communicating before the actual meeting can set you up to create a fantasy that he is more than what he really is."

To maximize success and minimize disappointment: *Stay in reality.* If someone seems promising online or even on the phone, by all means be hopeful. But don't marry yourself off in your head. A date is a date. You might have chemistry. More often, you don't.

A second or third date may look like the start of a lasting relationship. It may be. Or not. You can't prevent disappointments, but indulging in fantasies makes them worse.

One recently divorced fifty-five-year-old woman in New York was fixed up by friends with a charming, attractive businessman from Los Angeles who regularly came to town. He appeared to adore her, telling her how overwhelmed he was by her braininess and sexiness. She poured out her emotions, expressing the loneliness and disappointment she'd felt during her marriage. He seemed empathetic and caring. Three months later, he vanished. "I fell into a depression for weeks," she says. "I'd been lonely. I didn't realize how vulnerable I was." When she thought about the episode later, she realized they'd spent a total of thirty-six hours face-to-face. "He was a fantasy," she says.

It takes effort, but you can train yourself to stay in reality. Aleta,* sixty-one, did. Eighteen years after her divorce, she felt she could handle dating maturely. At the end of one lively coffee date, the attractive man sitting opposite her (now her live-in partner) said, "This was great. How about we have a real date Saturday night?" She said, "Sure."

"It gave me time to think," she says. "I didn't expect to be so eager." She practiced restraint. "I am going to approach this not just with my heart but with my head," she explains. "I need to *think* about what I might be getting into. That's the benefit of thirty years of experience."

She was surprised by her rush of feeling, but she relied on her judgment. After their first meeting, he was away for several weeks and they communicated by email and talked a couple of times on the phone. When he returned, she saw him about once a week. Meeting by meeting, she evaluated what she'd learned about him, where they were, what she wanted. After about six weeks, she felt more comfortable with him. Her head confirmed what her heart was telling her. This was a man she could love, who would be an equal and loving partner.

If you practice this kind of restraint, it will reduce pain and wasted time; and it will bring you closer to the love you want.

Chapter Six

Navigate the Emotional Currents of Dating

First Dates

Yes, it's an old saw. But you *do* have to kiss a lot of frogs to find your prince (or princess). Really, not even frogs. Most dates are fine people even without that magic chemistry.

If you feel a little nervous beforehand, that's okay. Like feeling anxious before a test or a big sports match, it can motivate you, shoot you with adrenaline and energy.

First-Date Dos and Don'ts

- DO try to look your best. You don't have to be thin, buff, or gorgeous to find a partner. But look like your best YOU. The effort shows. If you haven't changed your look in years, update it. One therapist pointed out to her freelancer client that

---

sweats wouldn't work on a date, and she felt hurt. Another woman told me she was grateful when friends insisted she get new outfits and *change that hair*! Now happily partnered, she says, "I'm glad I listened." If you haven't dated in ages, get advice. A widower in his seventies who'd recently lost fifty pounds got home from a coffee date to have his daughter exclaim, "Dad, you went on a date looking like *that*? That suit is swimming on you."

- Do NOT grumble about this upcoming date. If it's worth a meeting, it's worth showing up with a hopeful attitude and a smile.

- Do NOT get anxious because this could be the "one." Most first dates are one-offs.

- DO look for areas of common interest. Come prepared with an anecdote or two, a funny exchange you noticed on the street, why you're riveted by a novel about the Chinese Opium Wars, or your thoughts on *Game of Thrones*.

- Do NOT interrogate your date about previous relationships. If you'd like to dip your toe in, volunteer something positive about yourself and see whether your date reciprocates.

- Do NOT bring up political issues unless you're sure you share a viewpoint.

- Do NOT talk about your ex or late spouse.

- DO focus on what you're proud of or enjoy.

- Do NOT bring up your problems. Although you want to be authentic, don't bare your soul. That may make your listener uncomfortable. Focusing on negative issues is unlikely to show you at your best.

- DO be playful and flirt a little. Make eye contact and smile a lot.

- DO end the date on an upbeat note if you're enjoying it. If you must leave, explain: "I'm having a great time, but I have to be somewhere. Hope we'll see each other again."

- DO end the date early if you're miserable. Just say, "I'm afraid I have to go now," and, if you're at a restaurant or coffee shop, call for the check.

- DO be prepared to split the bill. If your date insists on paying, you can decide whether you want to accept or say, "Thanks very much, but I feel more comfortable splitting it."

- DO be clear if your date asks to see you again and you're sure you don't want to. As kindly as you can, say, "I've enjoyed meeting you, but the chemistry doesn't feel right for a romantic relationship." If your date presses to see you again as a "friend," be clear; I always said, "That's never worked for me, I'm afraid."

- DO send a warm signal if you'd like to see this date again, even if you're not sure the feeling is mutual. An inviting smile and saying you had a lovely time can encourage a shy person. You lose nothing if he's not interested. *But he knows I like him, and he doesn't like me!* Possibly. But you're not in junior high school anymore. You expose yourself the tiniest bit to someone you may never see again, and you up the odds he'll get in touch. If you feel the date is *not* going well, stay cheerful and know that it will soon end. In fact, you can end it any time you like. Just look at your watch and say, "Oh, I'm afraid I have to go now."

Harness Reason to Tame Dating Jitters

Are you nervous before a date? Imagine the worst-case scenarios: You'll make a fool of yourself? You'll like her and she won't like you? Your date will insult you? Possible but unlikely. At worst, you'll have an awkward conversation. You'll both be nervous. One of you will talk too much. One will be tongue-tied.

Or, miracle of miracles, you'll *connect* and talk on and on. Whatever you fear, you'll easily survive it. If there's no spark, even after all those promising emails, you'll be disappointed. So what? You've overcome many disappointments in your life.

If your anxiety paralyzes you so you can't even go on a date, here's a CBT strategy that can help. Set small, manageable goals. Instead of trying to meet the love of your life on a date, set an easier target: *I want to go on one date and live through it, however it turns out*. After that, aim for a more ambitious goal: to get through three dates.

I was in a therapy group years ago with a smart, attractive man who was terrified to ask a woman out. He feared a rejection would destroy him. The therapist gave him an assignment for the following week. He was to approach as many women as possible (at work, the supermarket, the gym) and collect ten rejections. Can you guess what happened? A few of the women agreed to go out with him. He did get six or seven rejections and . . . well, it just wasn't that awful. He still got a little anxious when he put himself out there, but he was never paralyzed by fear again.

During your date, stay in the moment. If you notice your own thoughts and feelings, you'll obsess less about your date's reaction to you. What is your date saying? Revealing? Do you *like* this person?

After her divorce from an insensitive, self-centered man, Bebe* dated men she met online throughout her fifties. During dates, she noticed not only how they treated her but also how they treated the waitress. She listened for how they spoke about their exes. One guy on a coffee date tossed off that his wife left him "just because" he used the kids' college fund to buy himself a Porsche. "I agree with your wife," she said, got up, and walked out.

"Get out of your head a little and pay attention to what you're feeling about him," advises therapist Osterle. "Your attention is your power."

What you talk about on a date depends on many things, but generally, you want to keep conversation light and ask open-ended questions. Don't drill down on whether she wants to marry. That reeks of desperation and negativity. Being desperate and clingy is the biggest turnoff on a date. And the biggest turn-ons? Displaying genuine interest in *him*, showing that you like *her*. Focusing your attention on the other person makes *you* look more attractive.

Life coach Treva Brandon Scharf, who married at fifty-one, dated desperately in her thirties as her biological clock sounded. No relationship worked. When babies were no longer feasible, she sought someone to *marry*.

"When I was almost fifty, I'd had it," she says. "I decided to give up, and that had to be okay. I can't feel like a failure. I decided to be the happiest single person I can be. I decided to be my own advocate and champion and the source of my own validation and self-comfort." Soon after this resolution, she met her husband, Robby Scharf. "I was relaxed and had no expectations," she says of their meeting. "I was just enjoying it."

Learn to Tolerate "Rejection"

You can be a champ at dating: realistic, charming, never fumbling. Still, some disappointment is inevitable. When you meet someone you like, you hope she likes you, too. After several great dates, if the guy takes off, it hurts. From the first email exchange to a first date to a fifth, the more you invest emotionally, the more disappointment you feel if it goes nowhere. If you've done the headwork to know you'll be okay, whatever happens, you'll feel a sting, then you'll move on.

Rejection hurts, especially if you interpret it to mean there's something wrong with *you*. Often it's *not* rejection. You and your date feel that spark or you don't. Probably neither of you knows why. There's good chemistry, such as the comfort and familiarity of being with someone who, like you, was the oldest sibling of a pack or another outsider inside corporate politics. Maybe his goofy jokes remind you of your brother. Maybe she finds your gap-toothed grin (like her dad's) incredibly sexy. Bingo!

There's also unhealthy chemistry, for example when you connect because her aloofness or unpredictability or some other not-great trait feels exciting. Believe it or not, your date may have been put off because you were *too* warm, too smart, or an altogether better prospect than he thinks he deserves. You'll never know why, and it's likely he doesn't know why, either.

Too often we torment ourselves looking for reasons. One seventy-one-year-old divorced woman in Florida took a "breakup" after a few dates really hard. She racked her brain trying to figure out *why*, what was *wrong* with her. A friend told her not to waste her time on why. "Just move on," she advised. Another friend, recently widowed, said, "You don't have cancer. Stop whining about a guy you barely knew." Soon she realized that guy wasn't important.

Don't Take It Personally: Consider Alternatives

As I've said, chemistry is mysterious. If you worry that something is wrong with you because someone doesn't reply to your email or call you, try thinking about it from another angle.

Temi,* now sixty-six and recently married, did this. After some online bumps, she responded gratefully to the "not interested" reaction. "Each person is entitled to want what they want," she says, "so when a man told me he wasn't interested, I thanked him for not wasting our mutual time. More often than not, a person who's not interested just doesn't respond. I mean, it's not the easiest message to share, even with a total stranger." When a man actually told her, she says, "I didn't have to wonder if the note got lost in the shuffle, if I should try again in a few weeks in case his decision changed."

If you persist in asking what's wrong with you, try this exercise: Write down at least ten reasons why this first or next date never happened, *all* having nothing to do with *you.*

Your list might look like this:

- Two days after he met me, he and someone he'd met before decided to be exclusive.
- She just wanted to get a sense of who's out there.
- He's scared to get close to anyone so soon after his wife's death.
- A crisis erupted with one of her kids.
- She doesn't feel a sexual charge with men who are nice to her.
- She decided that I lived too far away after all.
- That cough he had blossomed into pneumonia; he's in the hospital.

- An ex-girlfriend told him she'd like to get back together.
- He lost his job and is depressed.
- On vacation, she met someone she clicked with immediately.
- He realized the age difference was too big.
- She likes to keep her dates casual; I want a serious relationship.
- He's met thirty women in the last few months and can't find that elusive chemistry with anyone.
- He checks in to this dating site just for fun; he never answers emails.

I'm sure you can think of others. People are complicated. They have busy lives with many familial and other relationships. They have health problems. They have emotional problems. To assume there's something wrong with *you* is to ignore the reality of people's lives and the infinitely complex ingredient mix that ignites romance.

Cultivate Resilience

If you've been dumped, it *hurts*. So many now in lasting relationships suffered pain and disappointment while dating. They grew a thicker skin and kept going.

These are examples:

- A sixty-eight-year-old whose husband abruptly left her cried to friends the first time a man broke it off. "After that, it still hurt but less," she says. From then on, whenever she feared rejection, she'd tell herself, *It's happened to me before. I can be okay. I have a social life. I don't need a guy.* Six years later, she's married to a man who treasures her.

- A sixty-seven-year-old just-divorced man met one woman after another. "We had really nice times, but not one would have a second date with me," he says. Finally, one of his dates told him he was too raw to date. Six months later, he was fixed up with the woman he's with now. She's patient and loving, helping to heal his brokenness.

- One recently divorced fifty-seven-year-old woman remembers the first guy to tell her, "This isn't working for me." "That was *good* for me, to be broken up with and not be heartbroken," she says. Five years later, she married a man who adores her.

Every one of these people easily, if not painlessly, survived rejection. Each ultimately found a great relationship. Keep this in mind: You're stronger than you think. If you've survived divorce or widowhood, you've already been through far worse than having a brief relationship broken off.

As therapist Karen Osterle says, "Tell yourself, *I was okay before I met him. I didn't know him a month ago. I'll be okay tomorrow.*"

Find a Way to Laugh

Think of the profiles you scan, the emails you get, and the dates you have as an outsider might. Much of this experience is downright funny.

Bea,* a seventy-year-old widowed New Yorker, decided to take this attitude when she realized that for every ten notes she sent out, she got about two replies. *Huh,* she thought, *I guess I'm not such hot stuff.* She laughed. "I stopped taking myself too seriously," she says.

Since she was getting a 20 percent return on her effort, she figured, she'd write to even more guys. She had tons of dates, sometimes two a day. She felt as if she were seeing the whole human comedy.

She met guys who bloviated about their high school triumphs. Some looked *decades* older than their photo or alleged age. Others ruthlessly cross-examined her to uncover how she *must* be like their exes. She met sweet, lonely men who wanted only platonic relationships. Others mentioned Viagra within minutes of meeting.

She regaled friends with these stories, and they laughed with her. In one of her funniest episodes, she arranged to meet a man at a café only to find two men waiting for her. They were friends. "We both liked your profile," one explained. "So we decided we'd both show up and let you decide."

For Amelia,* sixty-eight, dating helped her laugh more than at any time since her husband took off. When she got a photo from a supposedly single guy who wanted to meet her, she laughed uproariously and sent it around to her friends. "He'd taken the photo of himself in his bathroom mirror, and in the reflection, you can see a bra hanging over the shower rod," she recounts.

She was also amused when the Italian American guy who treated her to two extravagant five-course Italian meals afterward wrote her a five-page letter explaining why he couldn't see her anymore. Before their first date, she'd explained that onions and garlic didn't agree with her. On that date and their next, he'd called ahead to make sure there was none in their food. They laughed and talked a lot at the table, but as he said in his letter, "I can't live with your dietary restrictions."

If You Spot a Red Flag, Learn More Before You Pass

It's good to notice red flags. Paying attention to potential issues can save you grief. On the other hand, reacting reflexively to stock situations can foreclose knowing someone terrific. Red flags are different from deal-breakers—for example, smokers, heavy drinkers, or compulsive gamblers. Red flags are not the same as personal triggers, like a susceptibility to controlling or repressed people.

Think of the light not as red but flashing yellow: *Proceed with caution*. If she's not available on weekends, she may have a good reason. If he lost custody of his kids, he may not have been a terrible parent. If you're nervous about someone not legally divorced, that's reasonable. But if there's real potential, learn more.

Not yet divorced was a definite red flag for Alana,* who met Bertie* when she was turning fifty. When some couple friends suggested she come to dinner with a pal of theirs, Alana said yes. She was intrigued by the possibility of male companionship, maybe somebody who'd go surfing with her. Before the dinner, she knew only that he was a bit older and, she assumed, divorced.

At first sight, she was attracted to his strong masculine presence. Talking easily at the table, she told him she'd grown up with four brothers. "He started teasing me," she says, "and that was it. He was *fun*."

He was attracted to her, too. Because he was living out of state, they exchanged long emails at first. Still, the red flag was waving. *Whoa! Whoa! His divorce has been put on hold*, she recalls telling herself. She learned it was because his wife, from whom he'd been separated for five years, was very sick. "It made me take a step back, though," she says, "keep it casual."

On their first real date, she says, "He laid it out there, who he was." He revealed how he'd once been a wealthy business leader and was now "humbled" by the 2008 recession. "He was brave about what he was looking for, what he'd hoped for and didn't get in his marriage," she says. On their next date, she summoned her courage and told her own painful story.

They took it slow. She reflected on what she needed in a partner now. In her thirties, she searched for someone to have babies with, someone successful and fun. At age fifty, with a business, two kids, and many friends, she wanted a partner who was smart, kind, responsible, adventurous, emotionally available, and honest. "I wanted someone who's *a rock*," she explains. In time, she found Bertie was that rock.

When I contacted her four years later, Bertie was long divorced. Alana sent me a breathtaking photo of them from the top of a mountain in the Himalayas. She joked, "We haven't set the wedding date yet, but we're trying out honeymoon destinations."

When You're Ambivalent, Keep Your Options Open

Being ambivalent about someone means you have both positive and negative feelings, often powerfully and simultaneously. The most sensible thing is to go slow, get to know her, and then decide: Move forward or away? Until you know, hold on to both possibilities.

Early on in dating, I was terrible at this. Often I acted out negative feelings without realizing it. Here's an example so outrageous that it was funny, even to me. I'd had a few fun dates with this man, then, after I became exclusive with someone else, I told him I couldn't see him again. No hard feelings.

A year later, when I wasn't dating anyone, he rode past on his bicycle, looked startled, and waved. Then I received his email asking whether I was available now and would like to get together. I wasn't sure. I sent his email to my friend Alice, asking whether she remembered this guy, and said I was hesitant about what to do. "I always felt ambivalent about him," I told Alice. Well, in fact, I was telling *him*. Instead of forwarding his email, I hit "reply all." He was not amused. Option closed.

In a more serious case, I'd had a six-month relationship with a brilliant, witty, but sometimes mean guy. I thought I wanted more commitment, but I unconsciously pushed him away. I let him know in ways large and small, including not being "in the mood" for sex, how he was lacking. When he broke it off, I felt hurt. It took some time and input from other people to realize that *I'd* pushed *him away*.

By the time I met Chris, I'd recognized this dynamic in myself. I became conscious of the signs of feeling conflicted. *Most* times I could manage not to act out. That was a very good thing, because my initial ambivalence to Chris was intense.

The photo he posted of himself in scuba gear underwater was meant to be eccentric, adventurous, and concealing of his true shape. I knew he had to be heavy, but I couldn't tell how much. He'd checked "a few extra pounds" as his body type. His writing was excellent. He was clearly intelligent and kind. And we matched on everything! We were both widowed nearly a decade, both single parents to kids about the same age. We'd both gone to graduate school and taught college lit (he was a Shakespeare scholar; I specialized in Victorian). We had many of the same books in the same editions on our shelves. We both wrote to earn a living. And we were both avid cyclists.

He was seated at the restaurant table when I arrived. I noticed his handsome face and broad shoulders. While I was an excitable little New Yorker, he was a large, calm westerner from Idaho. We had kinship and meaningful conversation about our similar journeys, the painful and the fulfilling. At times he wandered off into long stories about his father and grandfather tending horses on remote snow-bound prairies. On one hand, I was fascinated by a history so differ-ent from that of my own immigrant grandparents. On the other hand, he wasn't making eye contact and seemed not fully with me. Still, my overall impression was positive. Then, after the meal, he stood up and walked to the bathroom. Above the waist, he was broad-chested and full-bodied. Below, he was obese. I was shocked, a little horri-fied. *Red flag! Red flag! Red flag!* I'd been devastatingly widowed by a man I loved who had ignored hazards to his health. Also, well . . . I found his weight off-putting.

When I said good night to Chris, he seemed hesitant, and I felt conflicted. I'd felt a real pull toward him. He was smart, verbal, kind, loyal, a devoted father. We each understood what the other had been through and spoke the same language. On the other hand, he was clearly, despite a decent job, struggling to keep a roof over his kids' heads. He was a bit shabby. Sometimes he seemed a little disconnected. But most of all, that weight!

By the next morning, I still didn't know what to do. Maybe he wouldn't ask me out again. Then I received an adoring letter in my email box. He was utterly captivated by me. He mentioned the things I valued in myself: my strength through adversity, my intelligence, energy, and spirit. So we had a second date and a third, during which he was alert and fully connected to me. We had great talks and some really good times, although whenever he stood up and I saw all of him, I felt distressed. He looked so unhealthy. Could I learn to love a man in this shape? What were the chances that he could lose weight? On our fourth date, he told me he'd like to have a relationship with me. I'll tell you later about making that decision.

A Hard Balancing Act: Be Open and Vulnerable When You Don't Know How It Will End

How much should you open yourself to someone you're starting to date? What if, after a few increasingly intimate dates, you sense hesitation? What does it mean?

As you get to know each other, one of you might feel that the two of you are too different for a relationship to work. It's hard to find someone you can bond with despite your differences. This takes time to know.

Also, without an exclusivity agreement, either of you may be dating others. When things heat up with someone else, you can lose out. A sudden coolness can signal that your budding relationship is failing. Or something else entirely!

As feelings intensify, sometimes people need to pause. *Wait. What am I doing? I hardly know this person.* Maybe she needs to break off with others before feeling she can go to bed with you. Maybe he needs to think things through before committing.

Dan, a divorced man in his late sixties, was a thinker like this. He seemed enthusiastic about Dorothy, but after a few weeks, she felt a change. "The first few dates were magical, including our sex," she says. "Then he seemed to pull back." She wondered, *Is this the real Dan?* She tried to stay open to him, but she wanted to protect herself, too.

Dan later told Dorothy that he'd paused because he wanted his next relationship to last for the rest of his life. Dorothy might be the one, but he needed time to reflect and feel sure. A work trip to New Zealand gave him the space, mental and physical, to think about how they might grow together.

When he called her from there, Dorothy took it as a good sign. She was right. "When he came back, there was renewed warmth on both sides," she says. "He's cautious, but once he's in, he's *all* in."

If you've been dating someone and sense a change, you confront a challenge. If you ask what's going on, you might find out. But you run the risk of appearing to apply pressure. Not so good. Try to stay alert and notice what's happening. Don't overreact. Don't conclude. Is the change you're feeling about *you*? You can't be sure. If you're still interested, try to stay open and send positive signals.

It's hard to wait. But remind yourself that whatever happens, you'll be okay. Even if you move forward and date exclusively, either of you may conclude, *I gave that a try, and it wasn't right.*

Allowing yourself to be vulnerable can be challenging, but there's no way to know what a relationship can be without revealing yourself. And you may have to risk being the first to open up.

Roy,* sixty-one, had come through an anguishing divorce and knew he needed emotional honesty in a partner. When he met Wendy,* a divorced woman in her fifties, he shared his feelings early, what he'd been through and what he needed. She was taken aback. In her family, vulnerability was discouraged. The message growing up, she says, was "'Just get over it.' You never talked about needs or complained about hurt feelings." When he revealed his emotions so nakedly, she squirmed.

Yet early on, she had to choose. One night they took out their calendars to plan a date, but she couldn't find a time. "I had so many things down that it made me anxious to plan another," she says. "He closed his book," she recounts, "and said, 'Okay, let me know when you next want to get together.'" She could see he was upset. She went into another room, paced, and argued with herself. *This is a really great guy, and you're gonna screw it up*, she told herself. "I heard myself pushing him away. I realized if I wanted a relationship, I'd just have to figure this out."

Despite her discomfort, she admired his ability to be open and risk hurt. Inch by inch, she revealed her fears and needs and let him into her life. "He taught me through example," she says. "He'd be emotionally honest." She felt she had to respond in kind. "I tried to open up, and he met me with compassion and understanding."

She knows if she didn't allow herself to be vulnerable, hard as it was, she wouldn't be in an amazing relationship five years later.

Attracted but Unsure? Pace Yourself as You Date

What should you do when you like someone despite a red flag? Or when you're smitten but nervous? Go slow, go slow, go slow! Even when you feel only delightful chemistry on a first date, resist the temptation to see each other and talk constantly. Instead, give yourself time to think after each encounter. Stay with what happened, what you learned. Pay attention to how she reacts as you reveal yourself.

Therapist Mark McGonigle notes that his clients who take some time between calls and meetings, as well as texts and emails, ultimately fare better. The time apart is just as important as the time together. Ask yourself: What did you learn about him? What did you learn about how *you* are when you're together?

Two years post-divorce, Kevin,* in his early fifties, had learned to date cautiously. When he met Bonnie,* he was instantly attracted. She was completely different from his deceitful ex-wife and different from anyone he'd ever met. "She was flat-out honest, which is the number one thing for me," he says. "Also, she was super-smart and had done such interesting things in her life."

But. A big "but." Even four years after her divorce, she'd slip into tirades about her ex-husband and how he'd hurt her. "She was not healed," he says. "But she was so intriguing to me that I thought, *I don't have to make a decision now.*"

They waited six months before having sex. During that time, they got to know and trust each other. He helped her heal, he says. She agrees. Four years later, they got married. There are still moments when she goes off on her ex, he says. His response? "Enough of that."

You probably don't need to wait years. In the next chapter, I'll show you how to figure out your ground rules for a relationship, how to test whether it's right for you, how to move on if it's not, and how to move forward if it is.

Create a Relationship
to Cherish,
and Make It Work

Chapter Seven

Try a Relationship

Y ou've been dating someone for a few weeks, usually on a Saturday night. Are you in a "relationship"? Maybe yes, maybe no. That depends on your definition and that of the other person.

Many people think that once they've gone to bed, they're in a monogamous relationship. Maybe yes, maybe no. You have to check this out with the *other* person; the best time is *before* you go to bed.

Establish Your *Ground Rules for a Relationship*

Sex and Exclusivity

If you want to have sex with lots of people and are okay with your partner doing the same, that's fine, as long as you both accept the terms and practice safe sex. Most people with whom I've spoken are uncomfortable in a relationship that's not monogamous.

How can you tell whether he wants to be in a relationship? First ask for exclusivity. Then ask that you both get tested for STDs. This is a serious health issue (I'll talk about this in Chapter Eight). If he won't, you know he's not serious. How she handles your request reveals how trustworthy she is.

Saying no to STD testing, says Santa Rosa, CA, psychologist Carla Marie Manly, author of *Aging Joyfully*, is a "stop sign." "He says he adores you, he says he wants a long-term relationship, but you can't tell his real motives," she says. If he does agree, watch to see whether he follows through and shows you the results. If you already feel you can trust him, you may not need to see the results. But a willingness to show you is a good indication of sincerity.

Some people demand more before having sex. They want to wait for friendship to develop. Although some people wait much longer before having sex, most of those I spoke to moved faster. Demanding long-term commitment before bed probably won't work. After all, how can anyone commit long-term after a few weeks or months? You move from dating into a relationship to learn what it's actually like to spend exclusive time together. That helps people decide quickly when it doesn't work and when it does.

Catch and Release

At your age, you can probably tell soon when a relationship isn't for you. I suggest you *try* one because you can learn about it only by being *in* it. And what you learn can prompt you to end it immediately or to give it time to resolve your doubts.

Your age and experience are an advantage. "Older people don't idealize as much as younger people," says Tybe Diamond, a psychotherapist who works with aging adults at the Washington School of Psychiatry Center for the Study of Aging. "They usually have better skills at assessing who they're with."

As therapist McGonigle puts it: "Older people are better at sorting out the bad ones from the good ones. They get better at catch and release."

If you figure this out soon, don't hesitate; throw that fish back. But do it only if you're sure. Often this knowledge comes with a blinding flash of certainty. That was the case for a widow in her sixties just getting to know a new boyfriend. She noticed something strange. "He would always have to go to his car during dinner," she recalls. "I realized he was a closet smoker. Not for me." She didn't date smokers, and she didn't date dishonest men.

Sometimes you pick up more subtle signals. Meryl,* a widow in her seventies, for example, met Sol* online. From their first date, he kept her laughing for hours at a time. Over a couple of months, the laughs kept going along with some very good sex that had friends telling her she was "glowing." Then Sol's downsides got clearer. He didn't have the intellectual heft she craved, and although he wasn't poor and they split the cost of dates, she found him "cheap." Most of all, she says, "over time, he just didn't seem that into me physically." She'd noticed that he admired slim, boyish women. He was clearly smitten by that type in French films and when he noticed them at a restaurant or on the street. He seemed far less enthusiastic about her full-breasted body than her late husband had been.

"I asked him, and he admitted it," she says. She might have learned to deal with his lack of intellectuality and his frugality, but she would not submit to a relationship in which she did not feel cherished physically and accepted for who she was.

"It hurt to break it off," she says, "I won't kid you. But it also wasn't that big a deal. I'll live. And now I know I can do it."

Deeper issues tend to emerge with time. After six months of seeing a smart, successful man who wanted a serious relationship, a divorcée in her fifties intuited something disturbing. "Underneath, he was seething with rage," she says, "and he was so dogmatic about how people should behave. I asked myself, *Can you imagine* living *with him?* The answer was no."

If you feel that sure, break it off now. Don't make the mistake of hanging on because it's better to have *someone* than no one. Psychologist Manly sees this in the weekly women's group she runs, mostly with divorced women over sixty-five. Some are so needy they will continue in a relationship just to have *something*, she says, adding, "I support women to leave unpromising relationships." She helps them become stronger until they are less desperate and better able to find a fulfilling relationship.

For me, staying in a relationship that does not provide happiness and fulfillment is the ultimate definition of "settling." It has nothing to do with how attractive or successful or cultured your partner is. There's only one question that matters: Is this a healthy, sustaining relationship?

How to End It When You're Sure It's Not Right

Many people find it hard to break off a new relationship when they want out. They can't find the words. They worry about hurting the other person's feelings. They hope the other person will intuit their lack of enthusiasm and just go away.

Gail,* for example, a widow in her seventies, dated a man for four months. Sex was good, and talking was comfortable, but she knew it wouldn't work for her long-term. When he arrived at her place, he lacked interest or energy to do things she liked—for example, going to museums, theater, or concerts. He was crazy about her, and she enjoyed his admiration, but he just wasn't the kind of *partner* she wanted.

They met in June. By August, he was saying "I love you." She said nothing back. He asked whether he could call her his girlfriend. "I guess so," she replied grudgingly. "I figured he'd get the message," she says. But he didn't. When she went to Florida for the winter, she didn't invite him. "I figured our relationship would come to a natural end," she says.

It didn't. He called. He emailed. He suggested flying in. Finally, she had to tell him it was over. He was hurt and furious. He called her repeatedly that first week, upset and angry. He accused her of leading him on.

"I felt terrible," she says. "Did I lead him on? Maybe I did."

Because she was afraid to be direct, she hurt him more. When you know it's over, be kind by being *clear*. If this is hard for you, imagine yourself on the receiving end of vague hints and hurtful behaviors. Then summon your courage. Say kindly but firmly whatever your truth is.

- This just isn't working for me.
- I like you, but I don't feel love.
- I feel we're too different for our lives to mesh.
- I want things from a relationship that I feel I can't get from you.

When I broke up with Jonathan, a man I dated for three months, I asked him to sit down in my kitchen when he arrived. I said, "I'd like to talk to you, and it's rather painful."

"Is this goodbye?" he shot back.

"Yes," I said.

"Why?"

"It's just not working for me."

He wanted more details, but I thought he'd feel criticized if I specified. Just because he asked didn't mean I had to answer. I repeated that I was sorry, but the relationship didn't work for me.

He asked if we could stay friends.

I said, "I feel a clean break is better."

And that was that. I was free to date again. And so was he.

Be kind. Be clear. Free yourself and the other person.

You might at first miss her. You may find the breakup painful. But you will be able to move on and find the love you really want.

If Something Troubles You, Speak Up, Then Watch

Early on, you may notice something about your partner that's unsettling. If it's changeable, express your feelings and see what happens.

That's what Elise* did a month after Kurt* moved in with her. The two, both in their mid-sixties, had been introduced by friends. They clicked immediately, even on the phone. "Oh m' God," she says, "this man has a pulse and a sense of humor." When they met, he thought she was a knockout. They'd dated for three weeks when his lease ran out and she suggested they try being roommates at her place.

She was enjoying having him there when she noticed he had many intense late-night talks on the phone with his most recent ex-girlfriend. "He was still emotionally connected to her," Elise says. "I found that hard. I told him, 'That won't work for me. Make a choice.'" Kurt said he'd stop, but he didn't do it immediately. Elise told herself, *Let me monitor this*. If he couldn't do it, she'd ask him to leave.

Kurt found her demand reasonable but hard. He'd been with this other woman for years and was still in love with her. "I was trying to keep two balls in the air," he says. "Once she told me to choose, I did. But it took a couple of weeks to totally break off contact."

He never did move out—until he and Elise married and bought a house together.

If Something's Not Right, Ask Yourself Whether You *Are the Problem*

When you feel dissatisfied with your new relationship, don't assume *she's* the problem. Take a good look at yourself.

In her seventies, therapist Natalie Schwartzberg knew two things. It was hard to find a good relationship, and she was not always an ideal partner. This wisdom and self-knowledge, gleaned with age and experience, helped her save a promising bond. They'd met on a cruise and felt an instant mutual attraction. He thought she was gracious, funny, and smart. She found him brilliant, charming, and kind.

Yet early on, they bickered. They clashed over how much time to spend with his children and where to go on vacation, among other things. They compromised on trips, taking turns picking where to go. But they still squabbled.

Natalie often thought of ending the relationship, but there was so much good about it! Armed with self-knowledge, she examined her part in their arguments. She knew she was, as she says, "a big complainer." While he made himself agreeable during her vacation choices, on his, she groaned about the heat, criticized the food, and discounted the scenery. That annoyed him. So she trained herself to stop.

Another issue early on was that he sometimes didn't call when he'd said he would. She'd bring it up; he'd get huffy. Again she probed her part in these upsets. She realized she felt insecure with him and needed reassurance. But chastising him for not calling was counter-productive. Again she stopped herself. Over time, it sank in that he did love her, and the need to be reassured fell away.

The less she irritated him, the more loving he grew. Ten years after meeting (she's now eighty, and he's eighty-seven), they savor their love and companionship, emotional and physical intimacy, and fun. "The problems are so ironed out," she says. "I can't even think of the things I was annoyed about. No relationship is perfect, but we're happy in it, and that's the key."

If you become dissatisfied early on, reflect on what *your* role might be.

As for me, I know (and have been told often enough) that I can be bossy. I work at not being that way, but when I mess up, I apologize.

Look back on what you've learned about yourself in past relationships. Are you still (or again) slipping into those unproductive dynamics? Try making changes and notice whether your partner responds positively. If you have trouble changing, admit that you *recognize* this is *your* problem. That can help.

In her fifties when she met Roland,* Cecilia* had never been in a serious long-term relationship. She knew she wanted her partner to make her feel valued. She didn't feel that with Roland, and she thought *he* was the problem. "He did not make me a priority," she says. "And I didn't like the way he talked to me; he had a temper. Also, he said he'd never get married again, and I said I wanted that." After eight months, she broke it off.

A short time later, Cecilia turned to dating coach Sandy Weiner for help. When Roland contacted her, asking to reconnect, she considered it. He sounded different, she says, and he was willing to consider marriage.

Cecilia was also changing. Weiner was teaching her how to better communicate her needs. She realized she'd often sounded demanding or sarcastic with him. For example, when Roland planned a Saturday night with his kids, she spat out, "You care more about Saturday night with them than with me."

Now she'll say, "It would make me feel really special if you would make dinner reservations or get me flowers." She's also learned that when something she does triggers anger from his past, she can calmly point out, "I'm not that person."

They recently married. "Relationships are awesome, but they can take some work, especially in the beginning," she says. "Learning how to be open and honest in a constructive way can really make or break the relationship."

Test the Relationship Out

Okay, you're attracted from the get-go. But test it out. If you've been attracted to controlling people in the past, for example, notice how she reacts when you assert your autonomy. If past partners have met your needs with indifference or defensiveness, be sure to say what you need, and notice the response.

Ask yourself questions, like those below, that relate to *your* relationship history.

- Does he want to take over?
- How does she handle my anger?
- How does he react when I say no? Does he get angry or withdraw?
- How does he handle his own anger?
- Is she comfortable with me having my own life? For example, does she begrudge the time I spend with friends, family, or hobbies?
- Can he accept that I sometimes need to be alone?
- Does he reveal his feelings and welcome mine?

- Can he empathize with me? Or does he become stiff and change the subject?
- Must she always be right? Does she have trouble saying "I'm sorry"?
- Can he accept who I am with my vulnerabilities?

If you can be yourself without pretense and ask for what you need, you should find out fairly soon whether this is the right person for you.

Make Sure You Haven't Chosen the Same Bad-for-You Mate:

Identify Your Unconscious Agenda

It's hardest to evaluate a relationship that feels wonderful at first but then shows signs of an old toxic pattern. If you've repeatedly picked someone who's a narcissist, cheater, addict, or abuser, be vigilant. Is this new love like your old ones?

Do you recall this classic comedy skit by Robert Cook and Dudley Moore?

> *Reporter (Dudley Moore):* Do you feel you have learned from your mistakes?
>
> *Sir Arthur Streeb-Greebling (Peter Cook):* Oh, certainly, certainly! I have learned from my mistakes, and I'm sure I could repeat them exactly.

It may not be a laughing matter to you. But if you're repeatedly attracted to the same kind of partner, you must know it's not just luck. Your hidden antennae are leading you to these people.

So many experiences in your past affect the kind of mate you choose and the ways you act in a relationship. But if you're drawn again and again to a personality type that you *know* is bad for you, you're driven by patterns imprinted in you so early that you can't access them: They're *un*conscious. Yet, at the deepest level, they determine who attracts you.

There are various ways we learn to feel loved by our parents and, later, by intimate others. But when we gravitate repeatedly to a painful kind of love, that pull was most importantly forged in our earliest experiences as a baby and toddler of how love had to be, although our later childhood experiences have an effect as well.

As psychoanalyst Richard L. Rubens explains in *Polarities of Experience: The Psychology of the Real,* it is the *negative* aspects of the nurturing we receive from our parents that stamp in us an unconscious template for what love *feels* like.

If your mother was like mine—narcissistic and emotionally distant—she'll see you as an extension of herself and expect you to fulfill *her* needs. No matter how hard you try with your mother, you inevitably fail to do this. So she becomes annoyed, even angry, with you, and you experience a clouding over of her love. As a toddler, Rubens explains, you have only one choice: to assume that this is the only kind of love you can get and the only kind you *deserve.* You can't let yourself believe that she's a bad mother; you depend on her to survive. If she doesn't feed and shelter you, you'll die. Too scary to imagine. You've got to believe she's good and *you're* bad. At your core, being loved in this painful way *is* love. It's how love *feels* to you.

By age ten, you may be capable of thinking she's a really bad mother. By then, however, your experience of love laced with pain is part of you. The *negative* part of how she treated you is how you experience love. Later in life, you'll feel most comfortable on an unconscious level with someone who loves you the same way. I, for example, did not feel loved unless my partner distanced himself emotionally or got angry with me.

With someone whose personality is similar enough to the parent's, Rubens explains, "We feel a sense of comfort and safety: We feel we are relating to someone who is familiar in some deeply important, internal way; and we ourselves feel we can be someone in the relationship we are traditionally comfortable feeling *ourselves* to be." The problem is the part of our model that's based on a really *bad* experience, he says. This is the underlying negative chemistry that attracts us to problematic people.

This dynamic is hard to change, but don't despair. If you had an imperfect mother or father, that doesn't doom you eternally. Later experiences, later relationships, therapy, and other corrective ways of thinking can expand your understanding of love. (And, of course, it's my hope that this book will help you, too!)

The example I know best is myself. I've spent a lifetime figuring out what my unconscious template for love was. I wanted to experience love in a healthier, more satisfying way. Of course, I couldn't *remember* the ambivalent way my mother loved me when I was a baby. But I knew that deep down, I felt unlovable. I was an anxious, bookish child with few social skills. My mother was always shooing me outside to play with the other kids. Once I told her, "The other kids don't want to play with me." Her response was: "Why? What's wrong with you?"

Exactly. Something was wrong with *me*. Not that the other kids were mean, or cliquish, or that we had different interests. Little by little in my early adolescence, I made a few close friends and began to feel more "okay." By high school, I had some close friends who, like me, were studying hard to get into college. We told each other secrets. We loved each other. Still, I always worried that they'd stop loving me. When my best friend began confiding in another girl, I felt threatened.

Fast-forward to my twenties. I'd lost weight, learned to flirt, and had dates. I was interested in making conquests to prove men could be attracted to me. Until I met Alan when I was twenty-two, I'd had only one brief relationship, a summer romance with a boy in England. Alan was "appropriate," a recent graduate from Harvard Law School starting a job at a prestigious Wall Street firm. He was smart and funny and adventurous, and I enjoyed spending time with him. I had no idea I was "in love" until the subject of the "future" came up. I casually tossed off that I didn't see a future for us. His eyes registered shock and hurt, and in a whirlwind, he started gathering up the things he'd left at my apartment. He was leaving. For good.

Suddenly I was sobbing and begging him not to go. I loved him! I wanted him! He stopped packing his things and studied me. "I didn't realize how much I cared until now," I explained, still weeping. He relented, puzzled but relieved. A year later, we were married.

During much of the twenty-plus years we were married, I yearned for more passion, more of that "in love" exhilaration. Without understanding what I was doing, I started fights with him when he got home late from work. When he got furious and threatened to go back to the office, I would beg him not to go. And when he relented, I'd feel that burst of "in love" excitement. It was only many years after he died that I understood that to feel in love, I had to feel anxiety about being loved and a fear of abandonment. That was "love" as I'd learned it from my mother.

As Rubens explains, when we develop intimate relationships that repeat the negative relationships of our childhood, we do it in one of three ways. We find someone who will treat us as unlovable, bad, needing punishment, whatever feels like "love." Or, as I did with Alan, we provoke our partner into treating us that way. Some people pair up with someone unlike their parents, but they convince themselves that he or she *is* that way.

When I started dating online in my fifties, I said I wanted someone smart, verbal, and kind. I always found someone smart and verbal. Kind, not so much. My first relationships gave me the passion I needed because I gravitated to men who were emotionally unavailable. Their love always felt conditional. They kept me in a perpetual state of anxiety, which I experienced as excitement and passion.

In my decade of dating before I met my second husband, Chris, I began to look for more emotionally available men. I did much of the headwork I talk about in Chapter One. In particular, I worked on creating in myself a belief that I *was* lovable. I was in therapy and began to identify the signs of someone emotionally unavailable. By the time I met Chris, I'm happy to say, I found him exciting enough without needing to start fights. It took a while and a lot of psychological work, but it was worth it.

If you're still attracted to someone bad for you, don't be discouraged. Although you can't know what's going on in your unconscious, you can learn to identify the signs of a toxic person even as you're feeling that first rush of "love."

Be patient with yourself. If these relationships get shorter and shorter, that's progress, says therapist Russell Thackeray. "You're waking up sooner," he says. "Getting out faster is great."

Sally* has been getting out faster, but not fast enough for her. Now fifty-nine, she's still drawn to men who seem great at first; then she discovers they have addictive personalities.

She divorced her husband ten years ago. She adored him, and they had two wonderful children. It took her a long time to see his addictive personality. The pattern was shockingly familiar. Her father, who'd left the family when she was five, was a drunk. On his days with the kids, he'd come late or not at all. But he was a charmer. And when he did appear, he'd do something spectacular: Once he rented an RV and took them touring. When Sally was sixteen, he showed up with a car for her.

After her divorce, Sally's priority for a partner was "not my ex." She knew her father influenced the men she picked, but she couldn't identify the connection with the men she chose. After many lackluster dates, she met a guy who made her feel "sparky," a term she coined to describe a thrilling romantic charge.

This new man made life exciting. He'd wake her early on a Saturday morning and propose an outing: "Let's go climbing in the mountains." "He'd already packed a bag," she says. It took her a year to realize that he, too, was an addict: alcohol, weed, and cocaine. At first he'd kept it out of sight. Then he insisted on driving drunk. She ended it.

Recently, she met another man who made her feel "sparky." This guy lasted only a few months. By their fifth date, he wanted to move in with her. "When I told him things were moving too fast," she says, "he started ranting and raving at me. Then the scales fell off my eyes, and I realized that something was off about him."

Sally is discouraged, but she's making progress. Now she knows to be suspicious when she feels the "sparky" connection.

That frees her to look for a different kind of chemistry. When she reviews her history, she sees many "almost" relationships she broke off because there was something missing: probably that special charge that comes with the unpredictability and oversize gestures of some addicts. Without that feeling, she thought she'd be "settling." Moving forward, she's readier to find someone whose great qualities outweigh that unhealthy thrill.

"Sometimes people pull from the environment the exact opposite of what they say they want," says therapist Karen Osterle. "We're human, and we can't always see this in the moment. But what we can do is be on the lookout for another person's bad or undesirable behavior, notice it, and address it in a healthy, self-assertive way."

It's in the process of trying out relationships that you'll learn to identify these deep internal drives and to discover sooner: Does this prospect fit my well-worn but unhealthy groove?

How to Stop Choosing the Same Wrong Person

Ask yourself what your past relationships had in common. Look for *patterns.*

- What feelings did they arouse in you? Excitement and sexual attraction? A feeling of being rescued? A sense that you'd always known them?
- Identify common elements in their initial behavior, for example: pursuit, adoration, aloofness, intense interest in everything about you, sucking in *your* adoration and interest, desire to move fast, or discouraging of commitment.
- Make a chart of your major relationships. Create space for each of your responses to the issues posed above. List the similarities. As you meet new people, pay careful attention to things that fit the patterns.

This is the hardest part. Ask yourself what *payoff* you get from these behaviors. For example, a controlling partner might make you feel protected. Her coolness might tantalize and excite you. His overprotectiveness might instill feelings of comfort or safety.

Think deeply about these questions. If you're responding positively to negative behavior, as I've explained, this probably reflects how you were "loved" as a small child. You may make progress on your own. You may need a therapist to help you.

From your chart, make a list of red flags to spot and evade. If your previous partner was a narcissist, for example, notice whether your date asks about you and seems genuinely interested. Or does he talk only about himself? If your partners were liars and cheaters, be vigilant for inconsistencies.

Test out the relationship in the ways I suggest earlier. If you proceed in this measured, conscious way, you stand a better chance of not committing to someone bad for you or, at least, of breaking it off earlier. Then you can open up to someone who's *good* for you!

How Do I *Feel* in This Relationship?

In a healthy relationship, you feel good about who *you* are. If you haven't liked yourself much in previous relationships—have felt inferior or angry, for example—pay special attention to how you feel about yourself with a new partner.

Ask yourself:

- Can I relax and be myself, or do I need to present an acceptable front?
- Am I more accepting of my own (and my partner's) flaws than I've been before?
- Do I feel more confident and creative?
- Do I feel secure in his affection or do small things make me doubt it?
- Do I feel she has my back?
- Is our relationship deepening with time?

Does It Ever Make Sense to Get Help Early On?

Should you bother working at a new relationship when there are problems from the get-go? You may feel, with some justification, that at your age, a relationship either works or it doesn't. It's true that neither person will change all that much. We are who we are. Yet even if you can't change in basic ways, you can still grow. In fact, you're at an ideal age for personal growth. Seeing a couples therapist before problems get bigger can help you accept and work out your differences.

Therapist Stephanie Manes gives this example. A couple in their fifties shared many things. They both had a passion for music and art. She admired his creativity. He thought she was brilliant. But their worldviews and values clashed.

She was a successful executive, a high earner who measured success by money. He was a teacher and artist who'd achieved modest success: His paintings hung in galleries and sold. He was laid-back, content with his life and achievement.

They began living together in her luxurious home; she supported their lifestyle. She began pushing him to self-promote, make more money from his art. Her urgings just rolled off him, and she became resentful.

When they worked with Manes, the woman realized that what she really wanted was to feel taken care of by her partner, which she identified as his making more money. When he understood this, Manes says, he could hear it as a vulnerable need, and he looked for ways to make her feel cherished. He cooked for her, and he took charge of planning and booking their travel. He shared more about his work because she'd felt shut out of that world. In turn, she accepted his attitude toward money. After these adjustments, they no longer felt that something was wrong with their relationship.

If you and your partner have different approaches to lifestyle, money, or values, you can decide the relationship is unworkable. But if she has wonderful qualities, consider how you might accommodate your differences.

The executive and artist valued what they had enough to see a couples therapist. If you're uncertain but don't want to let go, consider counseling. It's not foolish or silly. You may have met scores of people, and this is the first one with whom you feel so much attraction and potential. Evaluate the "flaws" in that context.

No relationship is perfect. If much of it is good, consider tackling your issues immediately; find out whether you can resolve them. If not, you can part company.

It's not uncommon for couples just months into a relationship to seek counseling, says Ackerman Institute for the Family couples and family therapist Elana Katz. Most, she says, are having trouble talking about their differences and their capacity to deal with them. "If you've found somebody good but they have some rough edges and don't talk well, you may learn in treatment how to have more vulnerable conversations. I have seen people who want to get off to a good start to protect something precious."

As you work on the relationship, try not to be impatient. Ask yourself whether the relationship is *growing* in a positive direction. That's critical. Think of your intimate other as your "growth partner," suggests Chicago-area therapist Christina Vazquez, author of *The Uncherished Wife*; think of that partner as someone who can help you each develop a more mature self as well as a more fulfilling relationship. There's no better path to growth and maturity than a good relationship in which you can see yourself as you are and as you'd like to be. Even if it doesn't last, you'll be better primed for one that does.

You Think You're in Love, but You're Scared: *Take a Small Step — or a Giant (but Reversible) Leap*

If you're feeling really good together after a few months, one of you may be ready to move to the next stage. That might be saying "I love you"; it might be meeting each other's kids.

Are you frightened to commit even this far? Your partner may need reassurance that you're *in* this and moving forward. What to do? Review what you've learned about each other. Trust what you feel. Take that step. If it doesn't work out, you're strong enough to face it. Relationships either grow or die. Be brave and choose growth.

In her late sixties, Teresa* was afraid. Her unfaithful husband had left her ten years before. She'd had several relationships. Most recently, she'd been abruptly dumped by a boyfriend. Now she'd been with Keith* for six months. He was kind, patient, understanding, and affectionate. They could talk about everything. They could share their feelings, and he understood her painful history. He'd said "I love you" several times. He talked about a possible future together. Yet she hadn't been able to say "I love you."

When Keith first said it, she recalls, "I was excited and scared." He reassured her that he didn't expect her to reciprocate right away. "I didn't feel pressure," she says. "It made me feel love even more."

A few months later, however, he sat down with her in her kitchen and asked whether they could talk. He told her, "Every time I say 'I love you,' I hear silence. I know you were hurt, and it's difficult for you to express that you love me, but it's hard for me not to hear it. I wonder whether we're on the same page."

"I do love you," she said. "But I don't want to get hurt."

"I won't ever hurt you," he said.

She believed him. "Since then it's been great," she says. They've set a wedding date.

Not all promising relationships work long-term, but you can find out only by moving forward. Lawrence,* a divorced man in his sixties, recently took a huge leap of faith. When he met Cindy,* a widow his age, he felt an immediate sense of comfort. They had similar family and cultural backgrounds. She'd had a happy marriage, understood relationships, and was patient with him.

Six months later, he had to sell his house and find another place to live, and she suggested he move in. There was no "forever" commitment. Yet until the last moment, he wavered. Finally, he said yes. The week before the move, he called her. "I'm scared shitless," he said. "If you're not ready," she told him, "don't do this."

He had concerns, small and large, about living in her house. He didn't like her artwork, for example. "Okay, we'll negotiate that," she said.

"He's scared it won't work," she says. "I told him, 'Time will tell.'" She feels more certain they'll make it. She sees his moving in as a commitment. After all, she didn't pressure him to do it.

Several months later, things seem good between them. "We are learning more about each other as we live and share the same space, her space, full-time," Larry says. "After my divorce, I had become a real loner, enjoying my space yet feeling lonely at the end of the day. It sometimes leaves me a bit uncomfortable in this new relationship as my love for her grows each day."

He's not sorry he took the leap.

I've talked to other couples who jumped into living together early. In each case, it was a reversible step. There are other people in love—you may be one—who plan to live apart even if they commit to being together forever. It's a common choice for older couples, as is cohabitation without marriage. In a later chapter, I'll guide you through those relationship options, the emotional and practical benefits and drawbacks of each. You can choose what's right for you. You can negotiate the roles, structures, and freedoms you each need.

Chapter Eight

Rediscover Sex—with a New Partner at a New Time of Life

If you've found the one you want to be with, talk to, and hold close, you're poised to have the best sex of your life.

How is that possible? you may wonder. If you're a woman, your estrogen has all but evaporated, your vaginal tissues are dry and increasingly uncomfortable to the touch, you no longer lubricate naturally, and your libido is far from when a kiss could touch off a current of arousal. You're not as flexible as you used to be. If you're a man, your testosterone has declined. You're slower to get and hold an erection. You may or may not come. Loss of muscle mass or problem knees mean you can no longer have sex in all the positions you once liked.

You and your partner need to work this out *together*. So you talk more. You *collaborate*. You tell each other what you can and can't do, what feels good and what doesn't, what you need in order to get off. You're more vulnerable, more intimate, more *sharing* in your lovemaking than ever before.

Maybe when you were young, you had propulsive, passionate sex

147

that exploded in orgasm. Or maybe you had so-so sex, never feeling comfortable saying what you needed. If you were long married and raised kids, maybe you stole time for sex from the demands of work and children and running a life. If you divorced, you may have spent years with no sex at all. If you were widowed after a spouse's long illness, you may also have gone years without.

Did you start dating because you missed sex? Or do you believe your sexual life is behind you?

Whatever your previous experiences, whether you're fifty or eighty, you now have the chance to experience sexuality in new and deeply satisfying ways. Your age and maturity make this possible, as well as the depth of emotional intimacy you can bring to your cherished new relationship.

Some people want a relationship without *genital* sex, and that's okay. The important thing is to pick a partner who feels the same. As gynecologist and Northwestern University Feinberg School of Medicine professor Lauren Streicher told me, "Some people are just done; they're relieved not to have intercourse."

Whatever you choose (or whatever you can do), loving touch will still be a critical part of what knits you together and makes you a *couple*: sleeping in each other's arms, rubbing each other's back, holding hands, kissing. All of these are sexual. Never underestimate that.

Sex is good for your health, too. It boosts your immune system, lowers your blood pressure, and improves sleep; it reduces stress, depression, and anxiety. You don't need orgasms to benefit or, in fact, any kind of genital touch. Kissing, caressing, or sexy talk can set off your feel-good endorphins.

Before Sex with Someone New, Take Care

See Your Doctor

If you haven't had sex in a long time, be sure to see your doctor. Learn what's safe for you, what might be painful, and what you can do about it. Your gynecologist may prescribe an estrogen cream. Your urologist or internist may prescribe an erectile dysfunction (ED) medication.

One widow in her early seventies really missed sex. After ten fallow years, she was thrilled to start again. But she wished she'd seen her doctor first. The first time she and her new man had sex, she reports, "he had no trouble having an erection. I don't know whether he took a pill or not, but he went on for a long time. It was very painful, and I was bleeding like a virgin."

Afterward, her gynecologist prescribed a mechanical device to help her regain flexibility. "It didn't work for me," she says. "I waited too long. It's true what they say: 'Use it or lose it.'"

She found ways to please her partner, and he found ways to please her. "I enjoyed giving him pleasure," she says. "And I really enjoyed what he did for me."

Most doctors will give you a primer on avoiding sexually transmitted diseases (STDs). Many older people beginning to date, says Streicher, don't know you can get an STD from oral sex. When they were younger, they didn't worry about STDs, and many think they're too old to catch one. Using a condom isn't easy for older men who have trouble maintaining an erection. "It's a perfect storm for STDs," Streicher says. In fact, she says, STDs are rising faster among older people than younger.

Develop Trust

When you sleep with someone for the first time, you make yourself more vulnerable. During and after sex, love hormones flood your body: serotonin, dopamine, oxytocin. They create feelings of bliss and attachment. "After sex, a new vulnerability is present, breakups are harder, jealousies are more likely," says Yorba Linda, California, therapist Lois Nightingale. "The idea of the future is more pronounced and expectations are increased."

When you're older, you're also exposing your aging body, with its inevitable limitations and scars. Getting naked with a new person can be scary. You want to know your partner will be gentle and nonjudgmental.

Talk intimately before you have sex. "If it's too early in a relationship to reveal things you're embarrassed about, it's too early to have sex," says Nightingale.

When you have those awkward conversations, you want to know you can trust this person to be kind.

Have the Hard Talks

When you're about to go to bed, there are often things you need to discuss first. These conversations are rarely easy. On one side, they require courage; on the other, empathy.

These are some issues: Do we both want intercourse? What's possible and what's not? What do we each *need*?

People telegraph their interest in sex early on, even in their online profiles. If he says he loves cuddling but look elsewhere if you want more, you know what he's offering; he may be perfect for you. That's what a widow in her eighties wanted with a widower in her retirement community. They live in separate homes but see each other daily. Their relationship is filled with romance, flowers, wine, fine dining, dancing, and lots of kissing and cuddling. "My wife never liked flowers or romance," her partner says. "I'm so happy with her." What about sex? "Thank God we don't have to bother with *that* anymore," she says.

Between ages fifty and ninety-plus, variations in sexual interest and abilities are huge and not necessarily linked to age. An eighty-eight-year-old woman five years into a relationship with a man her age loves having sex. "You might think that at our age, physical intimacy is not important, but you'd be wrong," she says.

Many men start to lose their firm and frequent erections in their fifties. Some in their late seventies still get hard without drugs. Some work out at the gym regularly and remain strong and limber. Others have had heart attacks or respiratory issues and struggle to be active, both in the bedroom and out.

So if you're eager to be sexual, you're probably better matched with someone who speaks about passion and having a healthy libido. Yet even with eagerness, mutual acceptance of older bodies is crucial.

"The best way to deal with any sexual issue is to talk about it," says Philadelphia sex and marriage and family therapist Nancy Gambescia. "Get to know and trust your sexual partner before you have sex. Start with hugging and kissing and touching. You want to be comfortable with the person you're vulnerable with."

Talking first leads to better sex. If you're a woman anxious about whether it will hurt, if you're a man worrying about losing your erection, you're less likely to have good sex. "Distraction is a real sex killer," Gambescia says.

Reva,* seventy-three, was on her fourth date with a seventy-seven-year-old man whom she liked. She invited him in. After a glass of wine on her sofa, they started kissing passionately. That's when he gently broke away and said, "I need to tell you something."

He explained that because of a vascular disease, he wasn't able to have erections, but he could have orgasms. "I can't have intercourse," he told her, "but I can give you pleasure in other ways."

"That's great," she told him. "I can't have intercourse, either. It's too painful."

"He was very brave," she told me afterward. In fact, braver than she knew at the time. Later, she learned that a previous girlfriend had told him dismissively that, among other reasons for breaking up with him, they couldn't have "real sex."

Despite what they couldn't have—maybe *because* of it—these two worked out a satisfying and enjoyable sexual life.

Before You Have Sex . . . Talk about STDs

Some people reveal an STD on the first date. Others delay the safe-sex conversation until they can't put if off. They're at it hot and heavy on the sofa or in the car. Then one of them pulls away and asks the question or reveals the issue.

It was like that for Honey*and Raymond,* a sixty-seven-year-old divorcée and a seventy-five-year-old widower, who were on their fifth date. They'd already told each other they weren't dating anyone else and that they liked each other a lot. At a party earlier that evening, there'd been lots of touching and affectionate nudges, and now they were at her place, steps away from her bedroom.

That's when he interrupted their kissing and fondling. He told her he had herpes. "We need to use a condom," he said, "but I don't have one with me."

"I do," she said.

He was surprised but not unhappy. "She's a very practical woman," he says.

"I'm not a kid," she says. She knew she wanted to sleep with him, and she knew she wanted to be safe.

What if I Have an STD? When Do I Reveal It?

Before you have sex. That's a no-brainer. How long before? Some say to reveal your condition right away in case it's a deal-breaker for the other person. Some even mention it on their online profile! Others go directly to a site for people with STDs, like positivesingles.com or pozmatch.com.

If you wait too long, this way of thinking goes, you may get rejected after becoming emotionally involved. Others think you should wait as long as possible before having sex. Then, when you reveal your STD, the chances are better that she won't walk away, given how much she likes you.

As she dated, Ruth,* a sixty-nine-year-old widow, always waited until she and a man were on the cusp. But she paid a price. "With each new person, I felt anxious until I finally said the words 'I have herpes,' which I dropped in with a whole lot of other words about wanting to have sex and taking an antiviral drug so there was very little risk to him," she says.

Reactions varied from "That's fine" to "I need to think about this" to "Oh, no!" "Only one guy took off," she says. One got really angry when she told him after several dates. "He felt I'd deceived him," she says. "When other women revealed an STD up front, he'd told them it was a deal-breaker."

"We were sitting on a park bench when I spilled the beans," she relates. "He stalked away and circled and paced. After about ten minutes, he came back. He told me he really liked me and we'd work around it."

As long as you reveal your STD before you expose your partner, when you do it is totally your call. Figure out what you're most comfortable with. Or try it different ways with different people and see what works best.

How to Evaluate a Partner's STD

Not all sexually transmitted diseases are equal. Herpes, for example, which is very common, is an occasional annoyance for most people. It can be prevented and/or treated with an antiviral drug. Many people unknowingly carry the virus and never have symptoms.

Human papillomavirus (HPV) is also common. You can be symptom-free. Some types, however, can lead to genital warts or cancer. Like most STDs, it can be spread by oral as well as genital contact. When Honey and Raymond had been a committed couple for several years, they decided to stop using condoms; they avoided sex when he had a herpes outbreak. She did in the end test positive for herpes. More troubling is that she also developed HPV, which Raymond had no idea he had.

"I once had a procedure to try to get rid of it," she says. "That didn't work. I have to watch it carefully."

While HIV is no longer necessarily a death sentence, especially in first world countries, and, according to the Mayo Clinic, a daily pill can reduce your chances of getting it, it's still serious.

If your partner-to-be has an STD, ask your doctor about it. What you learn will help you evaluate whether to move forward. If you feel that an STD *might* be worth risking for the right person, try waiting longer before you have sex and get to know your partner better.

Adopt a New Model of Sex

Everything you ever learned about sex was based on how younger people have sex (if it wasn't totally mythical). That's because there just weren't many old people—period. Nobody, except maybe a few octogenarians, dreamed that the old could be sexual. The very idea was alien and off-putting. It's bad enough to know your parents must still be having sex. But your grandma? Unthinkable.

Now that so many of us are living longer and outliving our partners or our marriages, the idea (and practice) of sex for the old is out there. "We are all sexual beings from birth to death," says psychologist Rachel Needle of the Center for Marital and Sexual Health of South Florida. "The common notion is that when you are old, you don't—and maybe shouldn't—have sex. Yet older people are far sexier in both attitudes and performance than people think."

But here's the problem. In our culture, we tend to identify sex with intercourse. "That leads men of all ages to believe that erotic pleasure is located only in the penis," says Needle. When men have trouble getting and keeping an erection, even with Viagra or Cialis, many abandon sex. They've bought in to the myth that it's normal to lose interest in sex at a certain age. That's too bad; they lose out on a lot of erotic pleasure. Many also deprive their partners of the sexual touch they still crave.

When Elaine first met Howard, she rediscovered passion. "I thought I was out of business down there," she says with a laugh. They'd both gone years without sex. At first they had sex two or three times a day. "Unbelievable," she says. Later they had sex about once a week. Howard boasts of their freedom: "We don't have to raise kids or build a career. We can have sex any time of the month we want and any time of day!"

That was in 2014. Five years later, when I checked in on them,

Elaine told me they'd "lost interest" in sex. What she meant was *he'd* lost interest.

Howard admits he gave up on sex when he didn't regularly get an erection or feel he could stay hard. He's typical of an older generation of men who operate from an outdated model of what sex is, says American University psychologist and sex therapist Barry McCarthy, coauthor with Emily McCarthy of *Contemporary Male Sexuality: Confronting Myths and Promoting Change*. In this old model, McCarthy says, "The man's role is to perform for the woman by bringing her to orgasm either before or during intercourse, during which he comes inside of her. When he loses confidence in his ability to do this, even using ED drugs, he no longer wants to have sex."

Clinging to this model, many men believe the magic pill is the only answer to staying sexual. Even if their health permits them to take meds (and that may prove less feasible over time), they sooner or later become less able to "perform."

Older men need more stimulation to become physically aroused *and* emotionally excited, McCarthy explains. If they try to use that drug-induced erection too soon, they lose it. "Many older men try to go to intercourse before they're subjectively aroused," he says. "The Viagra erection isn't enough, but he's afraid of losing it if he waits. But if he's not aroused enough, he does lose his erection. When this happens, many men feel embarrassed and stop having sex."

Howard is typical of men so locked in to the performance model that they can't imagine an alternate path to sexual pleasure. A newer model, advocated by sex experts like McCarthy and Peggy Kleinplatz, University of Ottawa sex therapist and author of *Magnificent Sex: Lessons from Extraordinary Lovers* (with coauthor A. Dana Ménard), draws its strength from how we *change* as we get older. "The physiological trajectory of men and women converges with age," Kleinplatz says. Their similarity opens new opportunities for sexual expression.

"In this new model," says McCarthy, "a man doesn't *perform* for his partner. Whether you are male or female, you turn toward your partner and become intimate and erotic friends. Sex is not pass/fail. It's about having fun and touching and connecting with affectionate, playful and erotic touch, with or without intercourse.

"One of the great things about sex and aging," says McCarthy, who is seventy-five, "is that sex is more human and genuine." He recalls a couple he worked with who illustrate this attitude. The woman told her husband, "I like being sexual with you so much more now than fifty years ago. Then you had show-off erections. You didn't need anything from me. Now, in our seventies, you have grown-up erections. You need me more, and sex is better."

Ditch These Myths about Sex

Forget what you learned from your family, your friends, from movies, Catholic school, bars, or locker rooms:

- Sex is only for the young.
- Sex is only for procreation.
- Only the physically fit and healthy can have sex.
- Sex requires a man's hard penis.
- Without penetration, there's no sex.
- If you can't "finish," you shouldn't start.
- Sex should be spontaneous, not scheduled.
- Some sexual practices are shameful.

If you believe any of these things, think again. Researchers are finding that millions of people are having sex in later life. Many are enjoying the best sex of their lives. As one woman in her seventies told me, "The more comfortable we get together, the more adventurous our sex. It has an edge."

While drugs enable erections for many older men, couples can have incredible sex without an erection. They haven't given up on sex; they've expanded it.

Bad to schedule sex? Setting aside a dedicated time for sex increases anticipation, some couples say. As Laurel,* a woman in her seventies, told me, one of them might ask during the day, "You in the mood tonight?" If the answer is yes, or even maybe, each feels a pleasant tingle whenever the thought pops up.

A woman in another couple in their seventies told me they invariably have sex every Saturday and Sunday morning. "At first I felt a little hemmed in by that, but eventually, I started to be aroused just waking up and knowing he would be touching me," she says. "Mornings are actually best for me, but sometimes just for a change, I'll suggest we have breakfast and come back to bed later. Then maybe when he's reading on the sofa, I'll move his newspaper aside, sit on his lap, and give him some soul kisses. We still end up in bed, but with an exciting head start."

Rediscover Yourself Sexually

If you haven't had sex in a long time, prepare to be pleasantly surprised. It's easy to get used to going without, as I discovered after Chris died. The urge seems to have disappeared, you think. Then the right person kisses you or just looks in your eyes with desire, and omigosh, it's back!

In her research on older people in second marriages, University of Haifa social work professor Chaya Koren found this later-life re-discovery of sex not at all unusual. She tells the story of Hannah, seventy, who hadn't had sex in decades with her husband of forty-eight years. After she was widowed, though, Hannah told the researcher, "I discovered it interests me very much, and I didn't realize that this could happen in old age. But it was very intense." She had sex with two men she dated, just for the experience. When she met Dov, with whom she now lives, sex became new again. "It became something so beautiful, so romantic, so wonderful, it's really a kind of beautiful second chapter in life," she says.

If your marriage was sexless for a long time, it may take time to see yourself as a sexual being capable of both giving and receiving pleasure. If you've found the right person, start fresh. Don't make assumptions about yourself or your partner. Open yourself to new possibilities and sensations.

Develop Compatibility

Some people connect sexually immediately. It was like that for Honey (who had a condom when the right moment came) and Raymond. At seventy-five, Raymond is unusual in having no erectile problems at all. "I guess I take after my father," he says. In his nineties, his dad was worried that a procedure would affect his sexual functioning.

As for Honey, she says, "With a little lubricant, we're good to go. I feel we're like teenagers." Ten years after their initial sexual encounter, she says, their sex life has only gotten better.

Other folks have to negotiate their sexual compatibility so that it works for them. Or works *better*. With experimentation, most loving partners can develop an exciting erotic life with or without penetration. Both women and men say they just tell their partner what they *like* and move on from there.

At sixty-five, Diana* was shocked at how different sex could be. Long single, she'd had men in her life and lots of sex. It was exciting, heart-pounding, and fast. "It was all about f*cking," she says.

Until she met Ollie,* also sixty-five, she'd never been in a long-term serious relationship. And although she loved sex, she'd rarely had an orgasm. "I didn't say what I needed," she explains. "I guess I was too insecure."

When she and Ollie were about to go to bed for the first time, he told her he didn't always get hard, no matter how attracted he was. He seemed relaxed talking to her about it. This in itself was a revelation. She'd never *talked* about sex before.

As it happened, his erection was fine that first time. And she went at it with her usual frenzy. Too fast for him. "Her movements were so frantic I had trouble keeping up," he says. "The next time, she was sitting on the bed, and I told her I wanted to go slow. 'Let me do this,' I said. I started slowly undressing her and trying things out. 'Do you like this? This?'

"I wasn't in a hurry," Ollie adds. "We weren't going anywhere."

"He was so open in the beginning," she says. "He helped me be open."

Soon she was able to tell him that she was likelier to come from oral sex. He did it, and their sex got better. But it was the comfort and intimacy of their relationship that unleashed her orgasms.

She also had to learn what pleased *him*. He explained that he preferred her hand on him rather than her mouth. She wasn't used to doing that but found she enjoyed it.

"This is so much more intimate than any relationship I've ever had," she says. She can tell him that intercourse will be uncomfortable tonight because her bursitis is acting up. She can masturbate in front of him or he in front of her. It's all okay.

When Esther* fell in love with Scott,* both sixty-five, she showed *him* how to talk about sex. Widowed several years, she has found that her inhibitions about speaking out have disappeared. "At my age, if I want to say something, I'll say it," she says.

She and her late husband had talked about many things but never sex. Now she's freer. She asks: "What do you like? What do you want?" She's never had sex like this before. "I want to touch him all the time," she says. "I can't keep my hands off him. He says he's never had a woman that into him."

In fact, Scott had "never great" sex during his marriage and no sex at all the last few years. "When I suggested something to my wife, she heard it as criticism, and it made her feel bad," he says. "She refused to talk about sex, even in marriage counseling." With Esther, he says, "I've never had such open conversations. I can tell her exactly where and how to touch me, and she does the same."

If *you* want great sex, speak up. You probably know your body pretty well, what you *know* you like. But experiment. You may get over-the-top sensations you didn't know existed.

This was true for Holly,* seventy-four, now several years into a new relationship. She'd always liked sex, was usually orgasmic, and thought she knew her body well. "For me, it was always totally about the clit," she says. But when he stroked her in the folds around it, she flew into raptures. "Unbelievable," she says.

What *he* asked for was also new to her: to caress his scrotum. "Honestly, I thought it was strange," she says. She tried it, awkwardly at first. His ecstatic screams excited her: She experimented with little scratches, pinches, and pressing. "He told me I was the best lover he's ever had," she says.

"When we're done, even if we don't come, we snuggle into that post-sex bliss," she says. "Amazing."

Talk about Sex: Before, During, and After, With or Without Words

Saying what you want helps you get it, as long as you do it at the right time and in the right way.

- Talk before you get in the bedroom.

   Man or woman, it's better to let your partner know about possible issues ahead of time: "Won't get hard tonight, sweetie"; "Got a yeast infection, sweetheart." Over a glass of wine at the kitchen table can be good, or while taking a walk.

   Be reassuring. Say you'll enjoy being naked with him no matter what happens. Tell her you're happy to start and see where it goes. Suggest you have fun in whatever way feels good.

   That cozy cuddle on the couch can be a good time for requests. Ask for some small change, suggests Leslie Schover, a University of Texas psychologist and sex therapist at MD Anderson Cancer Center. "Let's make out here on the couch," you might say. Or "Let me show you how I'd love you to stroke me." Or "What would you think of watching a porno movie?"

   Rex* says he and his partner, Evie,* both just past seventy, would talk about sex when something on TV got them thinking. Sometimes the subject came up spontaneously. Sometimes one of them planned to bring it up. One day when they were reading the Sunday paper, he looked up and said, "How about we go to one of those fancy sex shops and just look around?" She was willing.

   It was a fun adventure and an "unthreatening" way to

discuss sex, he says. Evie recalls the toy they picked out, a penis-shaped rubber thing he wore on his finger. "It was quite satisfying," she says.

• Communicate inside the bedroom.

Talking inside the bedroom works, too, as long you're in the moment. In bed, the best communication is usually nonverbal. Guide your partner's hand to your penis, your balls, your inner thighs, your clitoris, your breast, your . . . You know the rest. Use words: "Quicker, slower, softer, go left, left, oh, *stay* right there: Don't move, don't move, don't move: *Now* move."

If you pay careful attention, you may not need words at all. Tune in to each other's breathing, rhythms, and moans of pleasure (or the occasional "ouch!"). "We know what the other likes," one seventy-seven-year old woman told me. "We listen to each other's breathing and reactions."

Never say what your partner does *wrong;* instead, say what you'd *like, how* you'd like it. If one of you feels uncomfortable about what happened (or didn't happen), don't talk right then. Avoid the awkward scenario in which somebody is apologizing. Apologies and good sex don't go together.

One of the wonderful things about being our age is that we're all changed and vulnerable in different ways, and neither of us has anything to apologize for. We just have to figure out what will give each of us pleasure. The more we make that a mutual enterprise, the better our sex and intimacy are.

At any age, couples can have what therapists call "desire disparity." You want it more than he does. Or he wants it more. Nobody is right or wrong. Do you recall the matched sequence in *Annie Hall* where Alvy and Annie are complaining to their respective shrinks about sex?

"We have sex all the *time*," she laments, "about three times a week!"
"We hardly *ever* have sex," Alvy grouses, "about three times a week."

When you're older and freer, you can work this out. You can help her come even when you can't, then roll over and nod off. Or vice versa. One of you can masturbate in the other's arms or lying next to each other.

Sex therapist Nancy Gambescia recalls a seventy-year-old husband who wanted sex more often than his wife. She liked sex about three times a week; he wanted it every day.

"I told him he was very *lucky*," says Gambescia. "I asked, 'Why does every orgasm have to come from *her*?' They worked it out."

Get Romantic, In and Out of the Bedroom

More than ever, sex isn't just about lust; it's about love. So *express* it. Use words, gestures, and tender eye contact. Kiss passionately. Snuggle in each other's arms. Text sweet or sexy messages when you're apart. Greet each other with hugs and kisses.

One sixty-eight-year-old woman does all of that. Since they live in separate homes, they're physically apart much of the time. But wherever they are, they feel connected. "We're more affectionate than I see a lot of young people being," she says. "When we're not together, we text morning and night and all through the day."

Couples who live together connect frequently in other ways. They signal passion with intense eye contact. They rumple each other's hair in passing. They rub each other's backs. And they say "I love you" whenever affection bubbles up.

Love builds to passion. It charges their sex and makes it tender. And whatever happens in the bedroom, they're in it together, even if they end up laughing: "Well, we gave that a try. Let's go to brunch."

Fixes, Workarounds, and Flights of Imagination

To have great sex after fifty, revise your expectations. Don't expect older bodies to act like younger ones.

You've probably lost muscle mass. Maybe your joints hurt. With aging, blood flow to the nerve endings in your genitals, male and female, decreases. Heart problems, high blood pressure, diabetes, and other medical issues impact sexuality. Some meds interfere with sex drive and functioning.

Men, don't be tough on yourselves or expect that you'll get it up immediately and then do it again ten minutes later. That's not happening. Women, if you're having more trouble reaching orgasm, find your way to waves of sexual pleasure that leave you sated.

"You're in a different body in a different time of life," says San Francisco area physiologist Fiona Gilbert. "Have fun. Embrace this. This is a whole new start of your life."

I say, use the changes in your body as a launchpad for creativity and passion. Enjoy lingering, creative foreplay for *both* of you. Touch the right spot on the ball of your foot and feel a charge to your genitals. Pull his earlobe down and release; hear a shriek of pleasure. Is there a spot on her lower back that, scratched lightly, sends her into ecstasy? Innovate. Try thumbs rather than fingers. Use your tongue in new places. Explore.

Try New Positions if You Can Have Intercourse

Maybe you loved the good old missionary style. Were you athletic and imaginative but can't bend yourself that way anymore? You can find ways to be sexy and *comfortable*.

A seventy-eight-year-old told me he couldn't manage his wife's favorite position because he had arthritis. She used to love when he stood and entered her from behind while stroking her clitoris. "I called that the contortionist position," he says, "but finally, I just had too much pain in my shoulders, even after piling up pillows. Now we're lying down, and my right leg is over her left leg. Then I can just reach down to stimulate her."

A seventy-two-year-old man said his "expanding stomach" required adaptations. "My new wife and I have found the best way is for her to be on top astride me," he says.

Women who want to be on top may struggle because of a weakened pelvic floor. Physiologist Fiona Gilbert teaches them exercises to strengthen their pelvic muscles.

Another couple told me intercourse works best for them with him standing on the edge of the bed and her lying there with her legs up. They got the mattress to the right height with bed risers. "I wonder what other sex toys you can find at the hardware store," she joked.

If you'd like ideas for new positions, take a look at the Swedish website Lelo.com. It shows diagrams of eight sexual positions for older couples that accommodate limitations due to arthritis, fibromyalgia, or other physical conditions. *Huh. I never thought of that one.*

In this context, I recall that old Ogden Nash rhyme "The Turtle":

The turtle lives 'twixt plated decks
Which practically conceal its sex.
I think it clever of the turtle
In such a fix to be so fertile.

Surely you can be smarter than the turtle. And not being fertile anymore makes for more freedom and fun.

When Erectile Dysfunction Drugs Are Great—and When They're Not

For some men, erectile dysfunction drugs like Viagra and Cialis are the answer. They can be, if you and your partner like the effects.

ED meds increase blood flow to the penis so that it becomes engorged and stays hard longer. They work only if you're *emotionally* excited. Some couples love it. Some women complain that the erection's too hard, lasts too long, and *hurts*. Some men experience unpleasant side effects like headache, flushing, upset stomach, and vision changes.

Some people prefer Cialis because it can last almost two days and allows more spontaneous sex. Viagra lasts a few hours. Some men say Viagra gives them a jolt while Cialis feels gentler.

If your doctor says you're healthy enough to take these meds and have sex, try one, and find out whether it's good for you both.

Experiment with Lubricants

The kind of lubricant you use matters. As Gilbert says, "K-Y Jelly isn't going to cut it. It's too sticky, and you want something more organic that slides better."

Your drugstore may not have the goods. Check out your classy sex shop or order discreetly online. You can get samples.

A younger friend turned me on to a whitish lube that looks and feels very much like my younger body's natural lube. It's called Liquid Silk, and I buy it online at Cheaplubes.com. It arrives in a nondescript brown box. The website is easy to navigate and offers subcategories: flavored, liquid, warming, stimulating, etc. I also discovered it comes in a pump bottle that's easy to use and fits comfortably in the hand, his or mine. As it happens, I like a water-soluble lube. When I tried silicon-based samples, they felt tacky to me.

Each type has advantages. The water-based washes off easily. To me, it feels smoother, but I do have to replenish it during sex. Silicon-based lubricants last longer, and some people prefer the way they feel. Try both. Shop online. Don't forget my personal favorites for all things sex: Babeland.com and Goodvibes.com.

Expand Sex Together

After your decades of growth, you're more confident, more comfortable revealing yourself and being bravely close. This capacity for intimacy can intensify your sex, as physical changes require deeper disclosures. The challenge is expanding your *thinking* about sex. You can help each other do that.

If You're a Man . . .

Men, you may find it difficult at first to let your partner touch and stroke or lick you anywhere but your penis. Until now, you've assumed that you need to give *her* foreplay: kissing, touching her breasts, stroking her clitoris.

After sixty, sex therapist McCarthy says, it's easier for women to become aroused and come than men. As a man, *you* also need foreplay. It may be similar: kissing, caressing, licking, touching—maybe in new places. Many men over fifty, for example, love having their partner finger or lick their scrotum.

Couples can create a more flexible and mutual sexuality by talking and experimenting. At seventy-five, John says he's experienced many physical changes. Earlier in his marriage, he devoted most of his efforts to arousing and satisfying Patricia.* "But now," he says, "I need more attention for me. It needs to be slow and gentle and not demanding of athleticism. I also need some kind of stroking, more prolonged and intense movement, and for her to play with my cock and balls."

What Patricia needs has also changed. "What gets me going now is having my right nipple stimulated with a finger, then with sucking," she says. "It's great if John's penis can be in me at the same time.

"Sometimes," she says, "we don't have enough energy to do it, so we just masturbate next to each other and hug. Or we help each other masturbate."

"At the end of the day, you want to be exhausted and spent, cuddling in your lover's arms," John says. "Who cares how you get there?

"Our sex now," he says, "is basically about sharing our emotional connection and reaffirming our love: *Wow, we're still alive and can enjoy ourselves.*"

If you haven't tried new things, you probably don't know what you're missing.

You can even become orgasmic in new ways. Not everyone knows, for example, that men can climax without an erection. Some men, insecure about their inability to get hard, resist believing it. They'd rather shelve the whole issue of sex.

Sex therapist Peggy Kleinplatz recalls one such man in his seventies. He and his wife were seeing her for help dealing with the sexual consequences of his advanced diabetes.

"He's lost interest in me," the wife said sadly. Her husband protested that he hadn't lost interest in *her*; he'd lost interest in sex.

"How do you know when you're interested in sex?" the therapist asked him.

"When my penis is hard," he responded promptly.

Kleinplatz asked whether there were other ways to know. For example, did he still get pleasure from oral sex?

"How do I know?" he said. "Why would she do that if I'm not hard?"

His wife's answer surprised him. "It's easier if you're soft. I won't feel like I'm choking."

Her husband still resisted. "How will she know when to stop?"

Kleinplatz made a suggestion. "Is it okay for her to give you oral sex until you say it's not pleasant?"

"I guess," he answered without enthusiasm.

Kleinplatz gave them an assignment for the following week: The wife was to give oral sex to her husband and see what happened.

Kleinplatz chuckles as she recalls their next session. The husband came in crowing, "Do you know it's possible for a man to have an orgasm if he's not hard?"

This couple needed a therapist to change their way of thinking about being sexual. There's a good chance you can help each other. It's often women who lead the way.

If You're a Woman . . .

Women have always had to be flexible. If you're a woman who's been orgasmic every time you've had intercourse, you're a rare woman indeed. You know what it is to need touch and other stimulation to get excited and climax. The idea of mutual stimulation, more give-and-take, is probably easier for you to accept. You may even prefer it to the old model and get off on arousing your partner.

If you can't have intercourse, ask for the kind of touch you like. Also experiment with sensations all over your body, places you don't usually think of as "sexual": your back, the crook of your knee, your toes. Urge your partner to explore any parts of your body *he* finds interesting. You may be surprised at what you find erotic. Even if you have trouble coming, you may experience erotic peaks that satisfy you.

You may have to overcome your partner's belief that sex is over for him by helping him expand his idea of sex. You're probably the only one who can.

He won't hear such advice from his male friends, if he talks to them about sex at all. He'll probably resist suggestions from his doctor, if he's lucky enough to have one not focused entirely on medical interventions. But he may very well listen to *you* if you gently show him how and make it fun. Think about what *you'll* get if he goes along with it.

Physiologist Fiona Gilbert has generally found men shyer about asking for what they want outside of intercourse. Many love massages. Some want genital stimulation but don't expect or ask for it. You may need to figure out what he wants or doesn't know yet that he wants. Be sure to tell him what *you* want. Ask him to try sucking your toes. Maybe it will be ecstatic. Maybe you'll giggle. Either way, it should be fun to try.

Improvise. Lick his nipples. Massage his fingers. One woman, whose partner couldn't have erections, tried something she'd never done before. "I told him I had a surprise for him," she reports, "but first he had to shower and wash all his orifices really well. When he got back to bed, I told him to lie on his belly. I was a little nervous, but he was really clean. So I licked him, as they say, 'where the sun don't shine.' He went wild. The next day he called me while I was out shopping and started singing that old R&B song: 'Fever, you give me fever . . . !' That gave him ideas about what he could do to me. All I'll say about that is 'Wow.'"

Add Zest: Buy It or Think It

Okay, you're older and can't do everything you used to. But you can do new things. Don't be put off by items called "sex toys." Maybe you think they're only for younger or kinkier folks. In fact, many are ideally suited to older lovers who need more stimulation. If you're turned off by the term "cock ring," know that some are identical to a device your doctor will offer as an "erectile dysfunction ring," which can be a silicon loop or circle that fits around the base of the penis.

It's fun to browse sex toys, online or off. Good Vibrations in San Francisco and Toys in Babeland in New York, for example, will welcome you with zero sleaze factor. Well-trained salespeople can give you professionally delivered explanations and answer questions. They also do this over the phone. Both have websites you can order from. Look for other options in your area. Check out toys like these:

- Vibrators. Lots of people enjoy using these in various shapes and sizes, made of rubber or other materials. Women find them a great path to orgasm; they can use them alone or with their partner.

- G-spot stimulator. Yes, Virginia, I believe there is a G-spot (I became a believer later in life), and a specially designed vibrator to massage that G-spot might help you find it.
- Tourniquets. Like cock rings, these can firm and preserve erections. You tie rubberized bands around the penis and scrotum, one or more according to what feels good. You can even buy medical tourniquets online; they're just like the ones that squeeze your arm when the technician takes blood. Don't use regular office-supply rubber bands. And don't leave them on too long. Ask your doctor what's safe.
- Pornography. This erotic category includes many different genres and comes in multiple mediums, from short video clips and picture books to full-length novels or movies. It's designed to spark your libido, whatever your taste. Bondage? Sex with strangers? Master of the manor seducing the parlor maid? It comes soft-core and hard-core and now includes pornography especially for women by women. If you like historical fiction, try Victorian novels such as *My Secret Life: An Erotic Diary of Victorian London*, *The Pearl: A Journal of Facetive and Voluptuous Reading*, and *The Romance of Lust*. They're all by that great writer Anonymous.
- Fantasy. Share fantasies. Or let your partner know you're in your own fantasy and ask him to help. I've found that men and women's fantasies can be different, and it doesn't always work to share them.
- Role-play. You can do this at home with no props, just using your imagination and playacting instincts. You can dress up. You can be more elaborate. I recently saw a British comedy

in which an older couple meets once a week as strangers. He offers her a lift, they flirt, and they end up in bed.

Sounds like fun to me.

When Infirmities Impair Your Sex Life, Accept and Adapt

When you find love in later life, you expect the usual run of afflictions: arthritis, stenosis, diabetes, heart disease, you name it. You're aware that one of you may get cancer. Whatever your medical condition, the illness or treatment can affect your sexual functioning. Many women and men are ill equipped to deal with these changes.

Prostate cancer, for example, is not usually fatal; it can be treated. But some couples are devastated by a loss of sexual functioning following surgery or radiation. Despite the claims people hear about the newest, latest noninvasive treatments, says MD Anderson Cancer Center's Leslie Schover, 80 percent of men end up with some sexual dysfunction. Many are disappointed and angry.

Some couples, even those who loved their sex lives before treatment, give it up. If that's acceptable to you both, that's fine. But some couples feel the lack of sex as a profound loss. Tina* and Arthur,* now sixty-six and sixty-nine, for example, experience their missing sexual intimacy as a shadow.

When they met, she was sixty-one and he was sixty-four. They felt an immediate comfort and attraction. They sped from first date to wedding in under a year. "Sex was great from the beginning," she says, "incredible and lovely."

It continued to be a deeply special part of their relationship until he got prostate cancer. After his treatment, she says, "Nothing worked." He can no longer experience intense sexual pleasure, she believes. So they have given up genital contact and rely on kissing and cuddling. She has felt this change as a "blow," and often when she lies in his arms, she says, "I see a deep sadness in his eyes."

I ask her whether he might feel sad, at least partly, because he can't please *her* sexually. Has she thought of asking how he'd feel about giving *her* pleasure? Would that make him feel better? Or worse?

"I don't know. We've never talked about it. We're both trying to protect each other. When there's something in life you can't change," she says, growing teary, "you let it be and make the best of it."

I feel sad for them and wonder whether there might be better ways to deal with it. Yes, say therapists who work with such couples. If the man and woman are open to therapy, says Schover, she explores with them what they consider acceptable ways to have sex. Some will venture out of their comfort zone; some will not. Both are legitimate choices. There are no shoulds.

Some men, Schover says, won't consider any sex without an erection. Instead they search out medical or mechanical solutions that don't always work. While men focus on their changed physiological functioning, women typically miss the affectionate and sensuous touch that often disappears along with intercourse.

"No matter what solution couples seek," Schover says, "it's important to do some sensual touching." She introduces couples to a twenty-minute exercise pioneered by Masters and Johnson in which each partner takes turns touching the other slowly all over their bodies except in the genital areas, at least for the first few weeks. "The goal," she says, "is to notice what it feels like to touch your partner. Over time, you add in giving your partner feedback on what gives you pleasure." (You can find a guide to these "sensate exercises" at Cornell Health: https://health.cornell.edu/sites/health/files/pdf-library /sensate-focus.pdf.)

Some complications of prostate cancer treatment are especially awful. Men can experience long-term incontinence or drip urine when sexually excited, Schover says. They feel shame and humiliation. If sex continues to be important for the couple, this condition is treatable, she says. For example, there's a penile implant that can be placed around the urethra; it allows the man to switch off urine flow during sex.

"This is so sensitive that couples can't talk about it," Schover says. "Many physicians are ill equipped to help these couples, and good sex therapists can be hard to find, especially outside major cities." She recommends the American Cancer Society as a good source of practical information.

Some couples move on to a nongenital era in their relationship. Some have conditions that make genital contact painful. Others, like Tina and Arthur, adopt this as their default position because they don't know another way.

If you and your partner have already expanded how you have sex, you'll probably find it easier to adapt as you confront illness. If you haven't, you can still learn this new kind of sex, when it will make all the difference between having sex and giving it up for good.

Reach for Transcendent Sex

In research to discover how to have "transcendent" sex in later life, Peggy Kleinplatz identified eight key emotional components:

- complete presence in the moment
- being in sync

- deep erotic intimacy
- communication with empathy
- being authentically yourself
- vulnerability
- emotional risk-taking
- openness to transformation

You may have developed these qualities during your many years of hard-won personal growth. They are areas you can keep working on, by yourself and with your partner.

For Better Sex, Keep Working on Your Relationship

Sex gets better as your relationship does. And your relationship deepens with your personal growth. Each reinforces the other. Below are some things to continue to work on:

- Communicate honestly and completely about your needs, wishes, and reactions.
- Allow yourself to be vulnerable.
- Feel empathy for your partner's frailties and your own.
- Allow yourself to be fully present to every sensation.
- Be alert to your partner's experiences in the moment.
- Learn your partner's body, desires, and limitations.
- Be willing to take risks, knowing that you'll be okay.
- Welcome change and adapt to it.
- Keep practicing, experimenting, and learning about sex.

Also, be generous. Give pleasure even if you don't want to take it. If one of you feels desire, it's okay to ask your partner to give you pleasure. You can do something caring and pleasurable in return: a backrub, a foot massage, cooking dinner, whatever would make your lover feel cherished.

Keep in mind that the deepest *intimacy* is between equals. So is the most passionate sex. When you love as an older person, you come together with past lives, relationships, children, careers, interests, and beliefs. You have a far better chance now of being an equal and independent person in your romantic relationship. And, within your partnership, you can continue growing as an individual.

What makes sex not only possible but amazing for older couples has little to do with the toll of age on your bodies. It's about the emotional connection between two equal and emotionally wise lovers.

Chapter Nine

Live Together or Not, Marry or Not: Create the Relationship You Need

O ne great thing about love at our age is the freedom to structure togetherness any way we like. We can live in our own
homes; we can spend as much time together (and apart)
as we want. We can live as if we're married but without the financial
or legal obligations. We can take vows but wall off our assets. Or we
can opt for a traditional marriage financially without traditional gender roles.

This ability to custom-tailor our union to our emotional, practical, and financial needs stems from major demographic shifts. Older
couples like us are "at the forefront of family change," says Bowling
Green State University sociologist Susan L. Brown. "Almost half of
divorced and widowed folks who form a union are cohabitating rather
than marrying," she says.

Many do marry, and a growing number of us have "living apart
together" (LAT) relationships: long-term, monogamous, and committed without sharing a home.

This wealth of choices, says University of Missouri gerontologist

Jacquelyn Benson, gives us new ways of "doing family." It goes along with major shifts in the U.S. and Europe, she says, "towards greater individualism, gender equality, and sexual choice."

Whichever we choose, we can have an intimate, loving, committed partnership for the rest of our lives. Each choice has benefits and drawbacks, affecting our sense of independence and togetherness, our relationships with family members and friends. It affects how we deal with financial differences and health issues. Most of all, the way we choose to *be* as loving committed partners lets us savor the sweetness of our love while minimizing potential sources of friction.

Chris and I contended with these options when we considered whether to marry. The subject came up dramatically after a mere nine months together. We'd just returned from a trip to Norway's Lofoten Islands, north of the Arctic Circle, during the season of the midnight sun. We stayed at an isolated farmhouse near a tiny village, with our bicycles for transportation. It was idyllic.

As we took this first vacation together, our children were not a concern. My older daughter and Chris's older son were independent. We each had a daughter in college, and his high school–age son could stay with a friend's family. Chris had a rambling old house in Brooklyn, an hour's subway ride from Manhattan. I had a large family apartment in the city. He was working as a writer in a financial firm; I was a freelance journalist, writing regularly for magazines and living partly on the assets I'd inherited when Alan died. I mention details like this because they *matter* when we think about joining our lives.

After our Norway trip, I was more in love with Chris than ever. It had been joyful to wake up with him every morning and go to bed with him every night. Back home, I thought how nice it would be if we could ultimately live together. His son had a year left of high school in Brooklyn; his daughter was only a freshman in college and was often at home.

So I was shocked by what happened the next week. We'd finished our favorite bike ride from Manhattan to Brighton Beach in Brooklyn and were eating at our usual Russian restaurant on the boardwalk. He seemed preoccupied. I worried that something might be wrong. After dinner, he led me to the rail overlooking the ocean and made an old-fashioned proposal. I remember the words: "You are the woman of my dreams." Then he asked, "Will you marry me?" I was stunned. Seeing how anxious he was for my reply, I said, "Yes," then quickly added, "But you don't mean right away?"

We waited a year. We talked and planned. How would we manage it? How could we make it work for the kids? We agreed to live in my place in the city. We consulted lawyers. Even though I'd said yes, we talked about whether getting legally *married* was a good idea. I had more money and felt it belonged to my kids. He was willing to sign a prenuptial agreement, which would also specify what money he or his kids would receive if he died first or we broke up. This was necessary because he was jointly funding the apartment renovation we were doing for our new blended family.

Suppose one of us needed long-term care? Without insurance, my assets would be decimated. We met with an insurance broker and bought two policies.

There were other financial issues. His daughter's scholarship was set, but his younger son would soon be applying for college and financial aid. Would my assets now be counted? I knew a financial aid specialist I'd written an article about, and we met with him. Although it seemed unfair to me, my assets as stepmother would indeed count. His youngest would receive no aid.

Chris and I went through the numbers. He really wanted to be married. I was hesitant about the financial issues, but I *liked* the idea. We were going to be a *family,* after all. So I made adjustments in how we shared living expenses to make it easier for Chris to afford tuition.

We hired a contractor to turn the tiny "maid's" room with bathroom into a loft bed/study for my daughter when she was home from college. With his son's input (dark green walls!), we redecorated the second bedroom for him. We built a Murphy bed in the dining room so that when his daughter was home from college, the dining table would move out and she would move in. My kids seemed a bit hesitant about their mom remarrying. His kids, who'd been motherless for nearly a decade, seemed warmer to the idea, although somewhat tentative.

We celebrated our wedding joyously with family and friends in our newly decorated home. The arrangements we put in place worked beautifully for a few very happy years. Then his lung cancer struck, followed swiftly by his death.

We were still a family. As the only living parent to his kids, I told them they were now "my children." I don't know how things would have unfolded had we not been married, but because we did marry, I was their stepmom. That's how they introduced me to college professors at graduation, to friends or distant relatives at the wedding where I walked my stepdaughter down the aisle, when I hosted my stepson's rehearsal dinner and my stepdaughter's baby shower.

Marriage was right for us then. If we'd been a decade older, maybe not. What arrangements will work for you? What will accord with your feelings for each other and your existing family obligations? What makes sense given your separate financial and real estate realities? What will allow you the freedom or lifestyle you need while satisfying your wishes for emotional and physical intimacy?

Think Through Your Emotional Needs

Many couples told me that their toughest decision was whether to share a home. Some felt strongly about marriage, yes or no, but the prospect of living together could be daunting. Some wanted it and glided into it easily. Some refused to consider it. Others took on the challenges of living together and negotiated their way around obstacles.

Before You Marry or Move in Together, Discuss Your Expectations

Some women resist cohabitating for fear of getting stuck in their old roles: cooking for him, doing laundry for him, and otherwise attending to his many needs. Nope. Been there, done that.

But now you can live together (if you'd like) in a new way. You're not raising kids, times have changed, and you have more freedom. But figure out what you *want*.

Ask yourself:

- What household tasks am I willing to assume?
- What social roles am I willing to perform—for example, arranging evenings with friends or planning vacations?
- How will living together affect my availability for the kids and grandkids?
- What time will I be sacrificing? What are the trade-offs?

Money

(See box: CONSULT YOUR LEGAL AND FINANCIAL ADVISERS ABOUT ANY CHANGE IN LEGAL STATUS)

- How much do I want to merge our money versus protect my assets?

- Am I willing to support my partner financially, partially or wholly?
- Do I want us to share household expenses?
- Does she have enough money to enjoy the activities I enjoy— such as eating out, going to the theater, or traveling. If not, am I willing to subsidize her?

Friends

- Do I want to see my friends on my own most of the time?
- Will I feel free to take trips alone or with friends?
- Will I feel okay if he wants to travel with his friends without me?

Activities

- If hiking or playing tennis is my joy, will I expect her to join me?
- Will I feel left out if he wants to take classes or play sports on his own?

Meals

- Do I want to get into routines where we usually eat together or eat the same food? Will I feel pressure to do so?

Talk about all this before deciding. That's best, but even if you don't, you can probably work it out. Many women are surprised by how willing their partner is to cook or clean. Many have learned to take care of themselves and even enjoy it.

After she divorced and forged a successful career, Becca,* a woman in her sixties, had no man in her life for decades. She met Josh* online and they fell in love. The idea of living together came up fairly quickly when he needed to move. Feeling brave and hopeful, she suggested he move in with her and see how it worked out. She had zero interest in the domestic tasks she'd performed in her marriage. As soon as Josh moved in, he looked around and said, "Where's your vacuum?"

"He had me at 'vacuum,'" she says. "The ground rules are different now. He told me, 'I don't expect you to cook for me.' We make more conscious decisions now about what roles we want, or we shed them. We outsource."

Take cleaning. She hated it, but she didn't want to load it all on him. She suggested they hire a cleaning person. He resisted at first, out of thrift. Finally, he agreed, and they split the cost. He believed raking leaves was his job, but after a few years, he was the one to suggest they hire someone. "I'd rather spend my weekend time with you than raking leaves," he told her.

How Strong Is Your Need for Independence?

At our age, many of us feel a powerful drive for independence, to control our own finances and major decisions. Here's the good news: You can build that autonomy into your relationship.

After her husband died, Brenda,* seventy-seven, craved solitude and freedom. When she met eighty-five-year-old widower Jerry,* they became a LAT couple, living in their own homes. "I liked living alone," Brenda says. "I didn't want to report where I was going and when I was coming back. I like going out with my friends often and going to visit my daughter."

Carmella,* in her late fifties and recently divorced, was high on her newfound ability to control her own territory and destiny. Throughout her twenty-year marriage, her husband had managed their finances and made the big decisions. Over time, she'd felt powerless in her marriage, especially in the financial realm.

"I couldn't wait to move out," she says. After the divorce, she moved into a rental apartment and restarted her career. Soon she was ready to buy a home, the first of her own. On her way to the closing, she says, "I had a turning point. It was the first big decision in my life where I didn't have to ask anyone or tell anyone. I felt: *I have power! I will take care of myself!*" She began singing on the street.

When she fell in love with Alex,* she felt happy and strong. Several nights each week he stayed with her. That worked. Then she became uneasy. He'd begun *assuming* that whenever he had to be in town, he'd stay with her. One night she blew up at him. "I love you, but this is my house," she declared. "You need to respect that."

"Are you breaking up with me?" he asked, alarmed.

"No," she said, "but I don't want to be in a *marriage*."

He backed off, and since then she has clearly set her boundaries, and he has respected them.

"My house is symbolic in my life," she says. "It's completely *mine*."

Many couples who live separately are heeding powerful needs, says therapist Stephanie Manes. "You feel it's *your* stuff, your house, your community, your friends."

Just past seventy and a couple for a decade, Lauren* and Christopher* feel living apart is the ideal framework for them. Neither was interested in marriage, but they quickly realized that sharing a home wouldn't work, either. Early on, when he had to move, they discussed whether he could move in with her. "The only security I had was my rent-controlled apartment," she says. "My stomach hurt when we talked about moving in together. Also, our styles and housekeeping are so different."

Lauren, fastidious to a fault, keeps her apartment looking like a spread in a décor magazine. "I enjoy setting a beautiful table," she says. "He'll eat soup from a can."

Christopher says wryly, gesturing first right, then left, "The world is divided into two: people who make their beds and people who don't. We recognized early on that we each needed our own place. De facto, we've worked it so I'm at her place two to three times a week, kind of open-ended, and she comes to my house about one weekend a month."

"We knew that if we lived together, we'd break up," she says. "This way, we always look forward to seeing each other, but we're not on top of each other at all."

For many later-life couples, that's the ideal.

Think About Caregiving Before You Commit to Living Together

If one of you needs long-term care, how will you handle it? You must discuss this. Women, especially, worry that they'll end up caring for a failing partner. Some spent years living what they felt was half a life as their spouse declined from cancer or Alzheimer's. They don't want to do it again. Other women fear ending their days this way after a few short years of love. Some people don't want a partner caring for them; they prefer to rely on their children, hire professional help, or move into assisted living.

Many believe that if they marry or live with someone, they'll be expected to assume this role. They probably will: The rub is that when you love someone, you may *want* to care for him. Living apart increases your odds of avoiding full-time caregiving. This is one reason older couples increasingly choose LAT. Research shows, however, that despite expressing a wish *not* to take this role, many partners *choose* to care for their loved one, at least partially.

Lauren, still working full-time, has long-term care insurance for herself. She never felt she could be a full-time caregiver for anyone. When Christopher needed major heart surgery requiring a lengthy at-home recuperation, they discussed it with each other and with his family.

"For two weeks when he was in the hospital, I was hands-on," she says. "Afterward, he stayed with me for several months, which was not a problem," she says. "Then his kids took over. I reached out to them and said, 'I can't handle this. I'm too stressed out.' We all pitched in."

Christopher is comfortable knowing that Lauren will never be a long-term caregiver for him if the need arises. As he reasons, "It's a much different thing to say 'for better or worse, in sickness and health' in one's twenties, when the idea is rather abstract, than later, when there might be a clearer reality of what particular 'sickness' one might need care for or be needed to care for. People might have a tacit commitment to care for each other. That's nice but probably should be addressed. For example, either of you might say to the other: 'It would be nice to have you here, but if I get to this stage, I may not expect you to stay.'"

Talk this over *before* you marry or move in together. "It takes *courage* to bring this up," says therapist Tybe Diamond. "But you need to say what you think and to risk your partner being upset with you." If you have trouble talking about these things, Diamond says, consider seeing a couples therapist briefly to learn safe ways to disagree about difficult subjects. They *will* come up.

Recognize that not everyone is cut out to be a caregiver, married or not. Diamond knows one married woman who agreed with her husband that, when he could no longer be on his own, he'd move into assisted living. His wife remained a devoted partner but not as a live-in caregiver. If you've ever been in an assisted living or nursing facility, you've probably seen lots of spouses visit, many for the better part of the day.

Most people over fifty who marry know that one of them may fall seriously ill; they're committed to caring for each other along the way and, if necessary, for the long term. That's also true of many who live together. For some, though, being thrust into caregiving can be upsetting. One seventy-four-year-old widow bought a new home with her seventy-nine-year-old partner, who was healthy, charming, and vibrant. Five years later, after a series of health crises, he's housebound and attended by professional aides several hours a day. She doesn't regret the relationship, diminished as it now is. She loves him and feels compassion for him, but she no longer has the life she wanted. "If I had it to do differently," she says, "I would not have lived together."

You may not know for sure how you'll respond if the time comes, but think about it and talk it over frankly with your partner.

Choose LAT to Insulate Yourself from Family Issues

Some family situations all but preclude your living together, at least for a while. Say that your mother, who has Alzheimer's, is living with you and becomes agitated around others. Maybe your partner's son, who's autistic, lives with him and functions best alone with his father. Maybe your mate's daughter, husband, and two children have moved in with him. Even if they'd welcome you, you may not want to live with them.

Before you live together or marry, get to know your partner's family situation. For clues, read Chapter Ten: Deal with the Kids—or Work Around Them.

What Does Marriage Mean to You?

What's the difference between living together and marrying? For many people our age, not much. Most older cohabitators are committed forever; they live and love as if married. Many would marry in a heartbeat if not for adverse financial consequences. Be sure you know what these are.

Consult Your Legal and Financial Advisers about Any Change in Legal Status

Marriage has major financial and legal consequences. Living together without marriage may also. Find out what they are.

Estate and Inheritance

- What must I do to guarantee that my children inherit my assets?
- If I live in a community-property state, how does marriage or cohabitation affect my bottom line?

Real Estate

- If I move into my partner's house, will I be able to stay after he dies?

- If her name is not on my deed, will that affect my homeowner's insurance?

Financial and Tax Questions

- If I receive support from my ex-spouse, how can I protect it?
- Will I still get my former spouse's Social Security or pension?

Health

- Will I be responsible for my partner's medical bills or debts?
- If she has to move into a nursing home, can I keep our house?
- If I need a nursing home, will I qualify for a Medicaid-supported facility?
- If I want my doctor to be able to discuss my care with him, what must I do?

Money issues keep many couples from marrying. But don't assume that cohabiting instead will fully protect you.

Take alimony, now called "maintenance." Most people who get it know that remarriage will reduce or eliminate it. But, says Chicago family law attorney Molly Sharma, if your finances are in any way "comingled," you can lose some or all of it. Courts have recently considered whether a cohabiting relationship is "marriage-like." To avoid affecting your alimony, take care not only to keep separate bank accounts but also to avoid joint memberships in a country club or other organization.

Although most states are not currently common-law, change is in the air, says Sharma. Make sure you have a cohabiting agreement on property so the house ends up the way you want after a death or breakup.

Some people want to marry. It's *important*. For Treva Brandon Scharf, marriage represents security and ultimate committed love. She'd grown up in an unstable home, searched years for love and marriage, and repeatedly been hurt by men who wouldn't commit to her. When she met Robby Scharf at age fifty, she was happily single. Everything was great between them. There was no rush and no strain. But when the subject of living together came up, she told him she'd never live with anyone unless they were married. "I wouldn't want to live together unless it's real," she told him. He immediately proposed. "I didn't want her to think I didn't want to spend the rest of my life together," he says.

If you live in a traditional community or come from a religious background, marriage may feel necessary. One newlywed in her fifties said marriage was her only option. Hers was a serious churchgoing family, she says. "'Living in sin' was unthinkable."

In areas such as Arlington, Virginia, where psychotherapist Jelena Kecmanovic practices, she says marriage is considered more respectable than cohabitation. In addition, she notes, some people believe that marrying is the only way their kids and grandkids will take their relationship seriously.

In fact, I recall several people telling me it was their kids who encouraged them to marry. These young adults felt more comfortable with a conventional relationship. A woman in her seventies living with her partner got this reaction from her daughter, who had a toddler: "My child is not going to call him 'Grandpa' unless you're married!"

Nora, sixty-one, and Will, sixty-eight, are a prime example of different attitudes toward wedlock. A couple in a small midwestern city, they'd begun dating (carefully, to avoid gossip) just months after her husband's death. A year later, when they were a serious couple, she felt strongly it would be marriage or nothing for them.

Unlike Will, she'd been very happily married. She'd been the first woman in her late husband's life. They'd married young, had three children, and loved each other for thirty-five years, until his death. Will, on the other hand, had one failed five-year marriage, many short-term relationships, and most recently, several years of happy bachelorhood. Will tried to convince her he was all in: forever! "It was a core feeling," he says. "This is the woman I need to spend my life with."

To Nora, his history seemed suspect. She suggested she move into his house for the summer as a trial. During those months, they fell into an easy routine. He did the cooking. She joined him on fix-up projects. They fitted together, sharing interests in politics, history, travel, and healthy living. When she moved out, as planned, she was willing to discuss the future. But what would that look like?

Will's history had made marriage seem irrelevant or worse. To him, a marriage license was a "piece of paper" that meant neither love nor respect. Nora felt differently. "There is something within me that says marriage signifies that you're in love and you want to spend the rest of your lives together," she says. She also believed marriage would reassure her uneasy kids that Will was truly committed.

Three years after their first date, he proposed. "I wasn't going to let my preference for cohabiting stop me from spending my life with her," he says. They signed a prenuptial agreement and created wills leaving what she had to her kids and what he had, except for his house, to his heirs.

Nora's happiness feels complete. She laughs, telling how Will acts surprised at the little things she does: giving him a backrub, telling him how handsome he is.

"Well, nobody ever did those things for me before," he says, chuckling. "I can't believe that the stars aligned so that I can be with this woman."

Cohabitating: Try It Out

Okay, you've decided. You want to share a home. Before you give up where you live now, try it! You know you're committed. What you *don't* know is whether you can share the same square footage.

You have long-engrained habits. You *need* some things a certain way. A few are hard to compromise on, says psychiatrist Ellen Berman—for example, the temperature at which you keep your house. Many older people, she notes, are extremely sensitive to heat and cold. "If he needs the thermostat set to sixty-five and you need it set for seventy-seven, no amount of sweaters will fix this," she says. If that's the case, hold on to your relationship, but keep your house, too.

"People can move in together too soon," says Washington, D.C., therapist Heather Williams. "They're surprised by how much has to be worked out because of sharing space. There are so many differences with just the habits of living."

Most people have to make big adjustments. You'll almost certainly bump up against issues that cause some couples to live apart. These include, among other things, differing needs for solitude and independence or an attachment to your own tastes and habits. You have a system for using your kitchen. He has no system and doesn't want one. The old saw about how you squeeze the toothpaste: That's a real thing.

Before you move in together, talk frankly about how you'll deal with disagreements. Because you *will* disagree. It's inevitable. You're two separate people. More important than any individual decision, says therapist Tybe Diamond, is to establish *how* you will talk about your differences. You might start a conversation this way: "We have to be honest with each other, and this will be hard," she suggests. "Couples can be afraid of hurting each other's feelings. Many don't feel safe arguing, but each needs to feel safe airing their positions, and this needs to be *said*."

Negotiate Where—and How—You'll Live

Ideally, couples start fresh in a home that's *theirs*. Even if that's possible, you'll still have to compromise from the get-go. When Carolyn Miller Parr, a Washington, D.C., author and judge, and her new husband, Jim Le Gette, a retired Secret Service officer, both past eighty, got married, they decided to find a house together. That wasn't easy. She lived in Washington and loved the city. He lived in the suburbs and hated the city. But they wanted to be together. So they compromised. "We settled on Annapolis," she says, "a nice little town with a lot of stuff going on."

For couples like them, location is the main issue. For Sharon* and Matt,* in their early sixties, the priority was minimizing friction over how they lived. After three years together, Matt was eager to live together. Maybe, she said. But never in his house! It overflowed with twenty-five years of clutter and was overrun by a ninety-pound furry dog. "I'm not a dog person," she says. "I hate poop, and hair all over my stuff."

(By the way, she's not the only one who put off sharing a home because of a pet. Another couple waited years. "He had three large aging dogs, and I lived in a no-dog apartment," she says. "We joked that we had to wait for the dogs to die.")

Sharon and Matt lived . . . uh . . . differently. He has hoarding tendencies, she says. "Once I tried to throw out a broken refrigerator magnet, and he wouldn't let me. But we got past all that. He's so sweet and loving, and we're both very independent and have lots of separate things in our lives."

The recipe for this bliss? Moving to a new house: the *right* house. They found a subdivision home that was affordable and large, with a spacious finished basement. Matt was happy to adopt this as his man cave, dog playground, and storage space for stuff. They agreed: He can keep it any way he wants and never apologize.

They share the two upper floors but under Sharon's rules: no clutter, no dog, no dirty socks on the bedroom floor. They eat and entertain together; they sleep and lounge together. When she's stressed, he helps and comforts her.

The upstairs stays neat. "He hasn't left his clothes all 'round once," she says. "I do what I want, and I don't have to go downstairs and look at his stuff."

If you can custom-tailor a new space to suit you both, great. But one of you may need to move into the other's home. Be aware: That's a challenge of a different color.

If you've invited her to move in, for example, be prepared to answer the inevitable question: Where is *my* space? If you're the one moving in, you'll undoubtedly want someplace that's yours.

When Robb* moved in with Rhoda,* he claimed the garage. She agreed. She helped clear it out, sacrificing her "cute white cubbies." "This is your turf," she told him.

Another question you may hear is: Where is *my* taste reflected? Before Paul moved into Virginia's house, this couple in their late seventies discussed what *he'd* bring. Her house was modern, modern, modern. She'd grown up with beat-up chairs and a sagging sofa. To her, "old" meant "poor." Paul, on the other hand, adored antiques: his cherry bedroom set, mission desk, and oak bookcases. "She's been great about being sensitive to what I treasure," he says.

The compensation for living with his old stuff, she says, is a partner willing to uproot himself from another state to live with her. "'Where you are is where I want to be,'" she recalls him saying.

"I want *him* to make this *his* house, too," she says.

How Will You Resolve Disputes?

At your age, you've learned a lot about constructive dispute resolution. You'd never say stuff like: "That's the ugliest couch I've ever seen!" Probably. Yet mature grown-ups like you can forget under stress. And make no mistake: Moving in together after being on one's own a long time can be stressful.

So, go back to Couples Communication 101. If you have something to resolve, ask whether it's a good time to talk. If it's not, set up a time that works for you both. If it is, calmly explain your difficulty. Use "I" statements, such as "I feel stressed by how much clutter is around." "I can't find a place to put my things down." "You" statements such as "You never put anything away!" ignite fights.

Imagine you've moved into his house. His favorite piece of furniture is a giant recliner in the living room, facing the television. You hate it; it's his favorite chair. Each of you needs to explain why you feel so strongly, what this thing *means* to you. Here's a model dialogue.

You: When I was growing up, my father had a recliner like that. Every night after dinner, he sat back and watched TV. He tuned us all out. He seemed to have no interests in life. I associate recliners with tired old people like my father. And I find brown leather ugly!

Your partner: Okay, it's not the best-looking chair, but it's *heaven* to sit in. I hate to tell you this, but I *am* old, and my arthritis tortures me. That chair is one of the few places where I can be pain-free.

You both have strong and valid feelings. Try to compromise. If there's a den or extra bedroom, maybe you can create a home theater for the recliner and TV. If not, maybe you can shop together for a recliner a bit more stylish but equally comfortable. If this doesn't work, weigh how much this one thing matters to you versus how much it matters to your partner. If you're the one with uncomfortable associations, consider your partner's physical pain. If you decide his comfort is more important, then just *let it go*.

It's amazing how much you can tolerate when the trade-off is an abiding love.

How to Manage Money When You Share a Space

Some who marry in later life follow a traditional path. One spouse financially supports the other. If this is you, I urge you to work out your financial understandings before you marry and to create a legal structure to cement them: for the children and the spouse, during the marriage and after.

Most couples I spoke to who got together after the age of fifty, whether married or not, do not pool assets. They're generally in the same age range; one or both have property or money that they want to pass on to their children. They consult lawyers. They draw up papers to cover all contingencies. For example, what would happen if you move into her home and she dies before you? "I told my kids," says one seventy-one-year-old cohabitator, " 'You can't kick him out or strip the home of stuff, even though the house is part of your inheritance.' " She knew that just telling them was not enough. She had her lawyer draw up documents to ensure he would be protected.

She and her partner did exhaustive financial research and agreed on a plan. They are among those who would like to marry but don't because of the financial consequences. She receives her ex's Social Security. Also, she notes, "marriage would be a big burden on me tax-wise." Because they live in a marital-property state, they own nothing jointly.

They do, however—like most couples sharing a home—split grocery and other household expenses. They don't fight about money. They follow these guidelines:

- Be realistic about what each of you can afford. If your income is similar, splitting expenses down the middle makes sense. If there's a disparity, one of you can offer to pay for the pricier things while the other covers more modest expenses. Even in LAT relationships, this comes into play. One woman in her fifties had more money than her partner. She bought some luxury items; he paid for other things. Example? "He takes me out to dinner," she says. "I pay for the Viagra."

- Be generous. It's common for the more affluent person to treat her partner to season tickets for the theater or baseball. If he has more, maybe he pays for vacations. It's a win/win situation because you get to enjoy these things together. The person with less money can be generous in other ways. For example, one couple splits their household expenses down the middle, but when they go out to dinner, he insists on paying.

- Be tolerant of each other's spending choices. If you share household expenses, you'll inevitably buy different things. Maybe you live on kale and cashews, while he breakfasts on Cookie Crisps and Oreos. Nobody wants to relive the college-roommate experience of labeling their food. As long as her spending isn't unreasonable, live and let live.

    As one woman told me: "We split our bills. He buys way too much beer, and I don't say anything. I buy way too many art supplies, and he doesn't say anything."

- When your partner spends his own money, even if you disapprove, say *nothing*. Never comment critically, for example: "I don't know why you guys went to such an expensive restaurant" or "You paid *how* much for that jacket? Are you nuts?"

Manage the Ghosts of Partners Past

If you want a new love, you can't populate your home with ghosts. Most widowed folks I've spoken to understand this. When they start dating, they usually remove the omnipresent signs of a late spouse. If you're ready to love again, you can't display that three-foot-high wedding portrait in your foyer to greet guests. I hated taking down the gorgeous photo of Chris (looking so handsome!) and me, but leaving it up would signal that I wasn't ready to move on. I do keep a few framed photos of Chris and Alan tucked into corners of my bookcases. They're there for me and my kids as part of our history. The men I loved and lost are part of me, but they are in my past.

More subtle signs of the late partner reside in the decor and use

of the house. Right after she moved into her partner's home, Louise*
was taken aback one morning while reading the paper on the living
room sofa with her feet up, sipping coffee and nibbling toast. Henry*
walked in and announced, "The rule in this house is we only eat in
the kitchen." His late wife's voice was ringing out clearly.

"That's not the rule as long as *I'm* in this house," Louise shot back.

"I never felt comfortable there," she says. "It was another woman's
house. The day-to-day decisions I was used to making myself were
now questioned!"

Before she'd moved in, the late-seventies widower told her he'd
let her make changes. Not true, she says. "He'd say, 'I'm sorry, but
that's the way it is.' I wanted a reading chair and he said no."

"Rocky" is how they describe their first months there. "We knew
we wanted to stay together," she says. "So we went to see a marriage
counselor. He learned he couldn't just say, 'This is the way it is,' that
we had to discuss it. Now we're much more collaborative. In fact,
he recently sold the house. We bought another one, which *I* get to
decorate."

He does want to make her happy, he says. "Initially, I didn't understand her wish not to live in my late wife's house. But I've learned
to be more open and to discuss issues."

Now just past eighty, they've been living together for six years.
Their love is special and fulfilling. But small things can still irritate
them. She likes to leave the lights on when she exits a room; he'll turn
them off. She gets annoyed to find all the kitchen cabinet doors open
after he's been there.

"I realized this was not a fatal flaw," she says. "When I thought
about things that aggravated me, they weren't so important after all.
The *relationship* was what was important. So I just let go."

Whether you marry, live together or apart, keep in mind how essential your relationship is to your happiness compared to anything else.

As one happily cohabitating woman in her sixties told me, "When we don't agree, we both back away and think about a different approach or change our mind. So much of what couples argue about is just so unimportant. Maybe, in a former life, I would have argued more. I think it's the combination of maturity and a different perspective on what's important—because of him."

Chapter Ten

Deal with the Kids—or Work Around Them

O ne of your biggest challenges as a new couple can be relating to the kids: your own and each other's. No matter how old they are, they'll have complicated feelings about your new love. Depending on your relationship with them, your family history, and their age and maturity, they can welcome your new relationship or threaten it. Ideally, your new love can be a force for good, bringing joy to your extended family and helping to repair any broken family relationships. If you don't have children or grandchildren of your own, your partner's can add a rich new dimension to your life. You have some influence over how these new family relationships unfold.

Discuss Family Expectations Early On

Discuss what you'd like with your partner. If your large, rambunctious family comes over regularly for dinner, you might imagine him pulling up another seat at the table. But he may prefer to take off when the crowd descends. Respect his choice—neither is right or wrong. Talk this out. If your grandkids live all around the country, would you rather visit them alone or with your new mate? What would she prefer? Talk it over.

Andrea,* seventy-one, lives with her seventy-five-year-old partner. He has no kids. She has three, and six grandkids she visits in different cities. Early on she asked him whether he'd like to come. He declined. She actually preferred that: She could spend more quality time with them. "He enjoys them when they visit, but in small doses," she says. "That's fine with me."

Move Slowly and Cautiously at First

With Your Own Children

If your kids have urged you to date, they'll probably welcome your new partner. Even so, they may not like him or want to see you often as a couple. They may resist his taking a paternal role with them.

If you've recently become single, your children may still be grieving the loss of their parent or the loss of their family as they knew it. They may not be ready for you to have someone new. On the other hand, if you've been on your own for years, they may also not like your having a partner; they may be attached to how available you've been for them. "They could experience your newfound relationship as a loss," says psychiatrist Ellen Berman. "They may not like the stepparent. It may be harder to go home."

You have an intense, complex history with your children. Your feelings for each other are primal. If they have unresolved wounds or anger, these will affect their feelings for you and your partner. When you introduce him to your family, go slow. However much you'd love to "blend" your new love into your family, it will take time. It may not happen at all.

Sound out your children. If they seem distressed, speak to them candidly as one adult to another. Listen carefully and acknowledge their feelings. Try not to be defensive. "Tell your child, 'I'm lonely and am looking for companionship,'" suggests therapist Lois Nightingale. "'If you have concerns, I'm open to hearing them. But I need to do what's right for me.'"

Carolyn Miller Parr and Jim Le Gette spent time hearing out their children about their intended marriage. Although Carolyn's first husband had died only a year before, she and Jim were both past eighty and felt viscerally that life was short; they had no time to waste.

Each had been a caregiver over several years. Carolyn's husband Jerry (the Secret Service agent who saved President Reagan from an assassin's fatal bullet, described in the Parrs' book, *In the Secret Service*) had declined from dementia. Jim had cared for his cancer-stricken wife. Like many long-term caregivers, they both mourned their spouse before death. They were ready to move on sooner than their kids were.

Some children in each family welcomed their parent's chance for happiness after so much suffering. Others found it painful. Carolyn's youngest daughter didn't say much when she heard the news, but, Carolyn recalls, "She looked like I had thrown ice water in her face." Mother and daughter talked a great deal. "Mama, I just feel sorry for Daddy," she once explained. Carolyn was loving and patient. She replied, "You know I didn't abandon your dad."

Although Jim's wife had died three years before, his younger children, now in their fifties, had seen their mother often. "It hit them harder to lose her," Jim says. "They were heartbroken."

"When children are still actively mourning their parent, they are not ready to let go of Mommy or Daddy or the way they see their parents," says counseling professor Allison Forti.

When Carolyn and Jim married in April 2017, all seven of their children stood with them in the wedding party. Carolyn's younger daughter, however, wept silently throughout. More than a year later, all the children have accepted the marriage and try to treat their parent's new mate warmly.

Although Carolyn and Jim planned to marry whatever their kids' reactions, they considered their feelings. Neither took the attitude: *You're a grown up! Just get over it.*

As you enter this new and potentially best relationship of your life, pay careful attention to your children's feelings. Do not assume because they're adults that your partnering won't matter to them. "It's a myth that *The dog is dead and the kids are grown: It's just us and it's our time,*" says Massachusetts therapist Patricia Papernow, author of *Surviving and Thriving in Stepfamily Relationships.*

If you're eager to get along with your partner's children, start by limiting your expectations. Remember, they're adults. They have or had mothers and fathers. They're probably not looking to you to play a parental role, although that may evolve with time.

This was the approach Marilyn* took. The fifty-five-year-old divorced mother of two married Ike,* a sixty-year-old widower with three daughters. She and Ike told the kids they were not expected to feel a certain way about their new stepparent. "I said to my girls," Marilyn explains, "'This is the man I'm with now. You have to develop your own relationship with him.'"

Over time, Marilyn's daughters, whose father was "out of the picture," have treated Ike more as a father figure than Marilyn anticipated. "But the dynamics were right," she says. "He is the only grandfather that my five-year-old granddaughter knows." Ike's daughters are cordial but more reserved. Marilyn accepts this, although she sometimes wishes they were closer.

Cordial is a good outcome. Even distantly polite may be acceptable. Some families experience hostility and conflict as a painful fact of life. Your children may be thrilled for you. Some may be devastated. Many will be ambivalent. Remember, no matter how old you are or they are, you're their parent forever.

How to Up Your Kids' Comfort with Your Partner

- Don't force togetherness; spend time together gradually.
- Let your children know they have a right to their feelings; you require them only to be polite and respectful.
- Acknowledge to them that you understand *change is hard.*
- Assure them you'll still spend time alone with them. Keep your promise, whether it's a drink once a week, a visit every few months, or an annual trip.
- Help them see that your having a partner benefits *them.* A happier parent, of course. Also less worry and responsibility for them. A mate who lives with you (and sometimes one who does not) can often prevent distress calls to the kids. One mom in her fifties heard her sixteen-year-old daughter say, "I don't dislike him; I don't want anyone in Daddy's place." This savvy mom responded, "You know, in a year you'll be away at college. If I don't have anyone else in my life, I'm going to be calling you every day and wanting to visit you every weekend." The young woman's eyes grew wide and she let out a long "Ooooh." She got it.

How to Relate to Your Partner's Kids

When you meet his family, be alert to how much you don't know. Do they have cherished traditions with their mother? Does his son distrust his dad's choices of women? Be aware that the kids may feel possessive or territorial. After all, they've known Mom or Dad all their lives, and you haven't.

An insider/outsider dynamic is common. The insiders have a shared understanding about "how we do things," says therapist Papernow. "You are a newcomer to a family system that's developed over decades and it will take you time to figure out."

If you're eager to get close, it's easy to overstep. "Maybe you are super-excited, but be aware this may be hard for his kids," cautions family therapist Tamara Statz. "Be yourself. Be open and show goodwill, but don't force yourself on them. You're there because you care for their parent. Maybe you can find out what you both enjoy about their dad."

It's easy to make mistakes with the best of intentions. For example, says Statz, suppose you offer to cook Christmas dinner and your partner likes the idea. But if his kids have developed a holiday tradition of eating out at their late mom's favorite restaurant, they may resent your taking over. If you err, apologize. You might say, "I'm sorry. I didn't know. I don't want to change how you do things."

Relieve Your Children's Inheritance Anxieties

A common barrier to adult kids accepting a new partner is the fear that she'll siphon off or swallow their inheritance. Whether they have a legal or moral right to their parent's assets is a separate question. If they've expected to get something, they can see a new spouse as a threat.

If you plan to leave your money to your children, as do most couples I spoke with, *tell* them so. Talk about your family's expectations in order to avoid problems now or later, says attorney Shawn E. Rosscup of Wells & McKittrick. "Sign a prenuptial agreement, and tell all the children you have one before the wedding."

When Marilyn married Ike, she had a glaring example of what *not* to do: When they married in their eighties, her mother and stepfather kept their financial arrangements a closed book, especially her stepfather. "In their generation, money was not talked about," Marilyn says, and she understood that. In the end, Marilyn's mother showed her the will, but her stepfather did not show his kids. "His children were worried about their inheritance," she says.

Marilyn has two daughters in their late thirties, and Ike has three, all in their twenties. "With my daughters, I set up a financial situation that has nothing to do with my marriage," she says. "I established trusts or bought life insurance to benefit them."

Although she encouraged Ike to do the same with his kids, he refused. He feels his financial situation is private. Marilyn is convinced that's partly why his children are still reserved with her, while hers have bonded enthusiastically with him.

If Your Child Is Hostile to Your Mate, You *Need to Deal with It*

If your sons and daughters angrily reject your mate without cause, their relationship with *you* is almost certainly the cause. Are your kids angry that you divorced their mom? Feeling betrayed because you left their dad for someone else? Maybe they're hurting because you weren't around much when they were growing up. Hear them out. Try to repair your relationship with them.

Consider having a few family therapy sessions with them. Just you and them. The issues arise from your biological family. You should address them there.

Psychiatrist Ellen Berman recalls one new husband's children both being angry with him and missing him. Their hurts from childhood remained "an open wound." In therapy with the father and his kids, Berman encouraged them to express their anger, their hurt, and their yearning. Over time, they repaired some of the damage, and in time the children welcomed his new wife.

Make Peace with the Relationships That Are Possible

It hurts when the children of the person you love freeze you out. Ask your partner whether you've offended them or accidentally touched on emotionally tender ground. If so, you can apologize and try to avoid touchy subjects. But don't assume they're reacting to *you*. Find out more about their family history.

After ten years of marriage, Bradley* still finds the sons of his wife, Roberta,* "very difficult to deal with," he says. The couple is in their late seventies. Her "boys," Tim* and Justin,* are in their forties, married with kids. Tim is civil to Bradley, but barely. Justin, he says, "has accepted me a little more, but as his mother's husband. We're not buddy-buddy. I wish it were otherwise."

Yet Bradley knows that her sons' reactions are not about *him*. Roberta's relationship to Tim is strained. "He's self-centered," she says. "He doesn't think at all about how others feel, especially his mom." He was very close to his late father, she explains, and he expects her to "sit home alone waiting for my son to call. Not that he calls much."

"I'm not broken up about it," she says of her boys' relationships to Bradley. "They're adults. I'm an adult. I don't tell them how to live their lives. They don't tell me how to live mine."

It's natural to wish your kids could see why you love this person so much, but that often doesn't happen. Noreen*'s son Tom* doesn't like her husband. "That hurts me at times," she says, "even though I understand why. My husband's an introvert, and he's unhappy in groups. I know he can be a grumpy old guy, but I hope that when we take care of Tom's new baby, those feelings will change."

Feelings can evolve with time and circumstances. But Noreen is realistic; she knows it may not happen, and she accepts it. By all means, work to make your family relationships warm and close, but understand if that's not possible.

If You and Your Partner's Child Clash, Work on Yourself First

You may be determined to love your mate's children: He dotes on his daughter; you *want* to like her. Because your wife sorrows over her son's pain, you want to empathize. Then, despite your best wishes, you can hardly be in the same room without bristling. What can you do?

Try first to work on your side of the relationship. Does his daughter remind you of your mother? Are you jealous of the closeness between your husband and his daughter? Does his son rub against old wounds?

Olivia is seventy-five* and in her second marriage. She regards herself as mature, insightful, and empathic—except with her step-daughter. "Over time, I grew to *hate* her," she confesses. They both grew up with verbally abusive mothers, she says. The young woman presses her hot buttons.

Olivia tries hard not to become hostile. "I remind myself that she's my husband's biological child," she says. "If my kids were the difficult ones, how would I want him to treat *them*?" She avoids sensitive subjects with her stepdaughter, and she never criticizes her to her husband. "Talking to him about it is the third rail," she says.

Marilyn made special efforts to placate her husband's daughters. She displays photos of the girls' late mother around their new house. "I was coming from my own mature and wise place rather than my younger, insecure, competitive place," she says. "Being as generous and thoughtful as possible is so important."

Doing this was harder for Lois,* who married in her late fifties. Her jealousy of her husband's daughters almost wrecked their relationship. "They almost act like he's their husband," she says. She's become aware, she says, that "you are coming into a situation that has existed long before your relationship did, and it depends on the children and their relationship with their father how it will all go down."

She's also learned to accept her husband's feelings. He grieved at how his divorce wounded his children; he devoted himself to making them feel loved and secure. Lois has learned to let him know what *she* needs without criticizing his parenting or his daughters. "I have had highs and lows here, and it has been the one thing that has been most challenging for sure. But it is good, and they are part of the package."

If Your Stepchildren Mistreat You, Limit Contact

If your situation with your stepchild is intolerable, limit your contact with her. Don't participate in casual visits, for example. When your stepson is present, show up only for important occasions or the occasional meal. Be guided by how unpleasant you feel the situation is.

Shelley,* a widow in her sixties remarried to a widower her age, took this approach to an extreme. During their engagement, his daughter said something that Shelley found unforgivable. She won't say what, only: "She crossed a line with me."

Shelley gave her husband-to-be an ultimatum: "I don't want to see her, to talk to her, or hear anything about her or her kids. If that's not okay, you can walk away." He thought for a week, then accepted her terms.

She knows this arrangement has hurt him, but she believes she had no choice. Having to endure her stepdaughter's abrasive presence would have added stress to her life that outweighed the benefits of the relationship. "I said to myself," she explains, "'I don't need this. Life is short.' I was prepared to give up the relationship. I know I should be able to rise above it, but I'm a grudge-holder. I know it's not a great trait, but that's who I am."

When her husband doesn't include her in certain plans, Shelley makes that easy for him. "I don't want to make him feel bad for going out without me, and I don't want to keep him from his kids," she says.

He's not sorry he agreed to Shelley's terms. "I feel a little sad," he says. "Every so often I get upset. But I still have a good relationship with my daughter, and I spend time with her."

"I look on the bright side," he tells me. "My partner and I have a great relationship. Last week we were at a concert when we heard this song." He begins singing: "'Night and day, you are the one, only you 'neath the moon and under the sun . . .' We grabbed each other's hands at the same time and smiled. We felt the *same*."

I'm not recommending Shelley as a model. Try to make peace for the sake of the person you love. Shelley could not. Her ultimatum was harsh, she admits, but it was the only way she felt she could keep this relationship they've both come to cherish.

Another drastic option is to live apart. Stephanie,* in a happy second marriage, was seriously considering this after two years of living with her teenage stepson. The boy had lived abroad with his mother and stepfather most of his life but had asked to live with them in the States for his last two years of high school. The couple had agreed.

"He was a very troubled child," she says, "and my husband was clueless about his son. On some level, it brought us together because we were both aggravated by him. When this boy walked into the house, it was instant misery and tension. There was a sense of doom around him."

When the son showed no signs of planning to leave after high school, she told her husband, "If he doesn't leave, I will. I can't live here with him." Husband and wife were on the same page. They got the boy therapy; they helped him move on and out. If that hadn't worked, she was prepared to keep her wonderful marriage, but from her own home.

When Divided Loyalties Challenge Your Couple Relationship, Resolve Them Internally and with Your Partner

Finding new love when you're older profoundly changes your life, mostly for the better. But when you add a new person to your family structure, it can shake up all the other relationships. Some that were central—a close daughter or devoted son, for example—may have to adjust to make room for your significant other.

It's not just your kids who need to adjust. If you've been that super-involved mom or grandpa, you may feel torn between your partner's needs and your children's.

Nina,* blissfully remarried, feels this tension. If time were unlimited, she'd attend all her grandkids' sporting and school events. She can't. "Why am I concerned about this?" she asks. "Am I worried about missing out on special times with my family? Or am I worried my family will be upset with me for not attending? Or am I worried that it appears to my family and the people in our town that I don't care about my family? Do people think I have abandoned my family and am self-centered instead of self-sacrificing? Argh!"

She suspects her children wish she could be more available. It's been five years since their father died. "It breaks my heart to think they would ever feel they have lost *my* love or interest in their lives. That would be like losing the other parent!"

If she hadn't married Eric,* she thinks, she'd devote more time to her family. But even when single, she knew she didn't want to be like women she knew whose whole life was caring for their grandkids. "I remember thinking I hoped my life would be fuller than that," she says. Now it is. "My husband understands my feelings, and for that I am thankful. Nothing can bring my first husband back. We both try to be great support for the kids and grandkids."

She rarely squabbles with Eric about this. He's quite independent and has many interests and friends. Still, when he's looking forward to an intimate dinner and movie at home and she gets a last-minute call to babysit, there's tension.

"They sometimes just feel they need a night out," she says. "I get that, as I'm sure I did that to my parents and in-laws, too, when I was raising my kids." Eric, who has no kids of his own, admits that while she sometimes turns down those last-minute requests because of him, sometimes she doesn't. "If I wanted a quiet evening with her, it does bother me," he says.

He lives with the frustration. She lives with the angst.

"Divided loyalties are nearly universal," says psychiatrist Berman. Why? You want to please people you love who want different things. Noreen, for example, is often caught between trying to please her husband *and* her kids. Her boys love trendy restaurants that sound like a party at full volume. Her husband can't stand them. The din bothers her less. When they celebrate her son's birthday, she lets him pick the restaurant. Secretly, she wants to side with her son: "I want to throw my husband under the bus and say, 'You know he can't stand noisy places,'" she admits. She's taught herself to say, "*We'd* prefer a somewhat quieter place." Still, when they're eating and have to shout to hear each other, she says, "I can feel the tension."

Do You Need to Alter Long-Established Boundaries?

Your bond with your kids has to affect your couple relationship. A lot depends on the boundaries you've established with them earlier. Are you used to seeing them every day? Do you vacation together? Does your son still lean on you for help when he's capable of being more independent?

Whatever your previous boundaries, when you shift to being half of a couple, your earth will rumble. The tremors may be barely noticeable or may threaten your relationship.

Think of this story as archetypal. Therapist Pat Papernow told me it combines many stories. Here's one version. A newly married couple, much in love, move into her house. She's raised her children there, several of whom live nearby. It's a lovely home with lots of room for a couple.

One day when the husband is home alone, maybe sitting in his favorite chair and enjoying the crossword puzzle, he hears a key turn in the lock. His wife's oldest daughter waves at him, then marches into the kitchen and starts opening cabinets, looking for some ingredients she needs. He's appalled at this violation of his privacy. This is *his* house and his wife's. It's *not* okay for the kids to wander in any time they want.

When he tells his wife, which he does in the strongest terms, she sees the situation differently. "This is my children's home," she says. "They grew up here. They've had keys all their lives and have always felt free to pop in and out. How can I take their keys away? What would I be saying to them, that they're not my kids anymore, that this is no longer their home?"

Both felt so strongly that they turned to Papernow. What she helped them do is what you need to do if you find yourself in a similar conflict. Understand the depth of your mate's feelings and empathize. Understand that you feel differently, but neither is right, and neither is wrong. Recognize that what you're asking, something sensible and straightforward to you, is anything but for your partner. Be aware, says Papernow, that "it's a huge change for the adult children. Suddenly, their parent wants a boundary that was never there before."

If you're in the husband's position and feel the daughter's behavior is a violation, understand this: You've entered a family system that's existed for decades. Its latest version, created when your wife's marriage ended, has evolved over years. This is *the way things have always been* between this mother and her children. Recognize that if your wife *can* ask her daughters for the keys, it will cost her emotionally. She'll have to initiate a painful discussion with them. She'll need to admit she's asking for a big change that's very hard. She'll have to hear their grief and anger.

"Who wants to hear that their adult kids are not happy that she's happy?" Papernow says. "But if you're the kids, can you imagine that you have always had the keys to the house and now you have to give them up? They are part of the rituals of how you are together. Changing this is a *loss* for them."

If you're in the wife's position, try to understand how intrusive these behaviors are for your partner. Your couple relationship and your parent/child relationship are both central; they both need to work. You don't have to resolve all boundary issues. If your mate can't set limits with his kids, you may find his behavior merely irritating. Try to live with it.

"Stepparents always want more limits and boundaries with the kids," says Papernow. "Parents want the stepparents to *understand* their kids. This takes time to work out. Couples need to hear each other across their differences. With time and constructive dialogue, parents can help stepparents be less judgmental; stepparents can show parents where changes would be good."

Wayne,* a widower of seventy, is in a LAT relationship with Rosemary,* a divorcée a few years younger. For several years running, she watched him cope with exhausting visits from his adult son and daughter-in-law. Because Wayne lived in a resort area, his son used the house as a free vacation spot for himself, his wife, and another couple. On holiday weekends when they came, the four got roaring drunk, littering the house with empty bottles and making life intolerable for Wayne. Wayne saw his son's alcohol problem as rooted in his mother's death and felt stricken for him. He was also afraid to come down hard on him, fearing he'd see him less.

Rosemary told him he was letting himself get beat up emotionally. She empathized with his fears. But after one rowdy dinner with this crew, she told Wayne she wouldn't do *that* again.

Over time, Wayne looked to her for advice. With her encouragement, Wayne called his son. He had trouble getting the words out, but he did say that he couldn't handle the alcohol-fueled behavior. He empathized with his son's pain and told him that he was glad to have him over, but the other couple was not welcome. When his son and daughter-in-law came next, they came on their own, drank less, and behaved better.

It's not easy for couples to talk about their own or their partner's kids. If you think her kids are taking advantage of or being disrespectful to him, it's upsetting. You're angry with the kids; you're critical of your partner's parenting *and* concerned for him.

One couple in their eighties, remarried after being widowed, argued over the wife's daughter. From childhood on, she'd struggled with mental health issues. As an adult, she was very dependent on her mother. Her stepfather saw her as taking advantage of her mother. "He felt caught between being supportive of his wife and angry with the daughter," says Kathryn Chefetz, a psychoanalyst in the aging program at the Washington School of Psychiatry.

In therapy, the wife saw that she needed to establish limits with her daughter. Her husband learned to empathize with his wife's sorrow over her daughter's challenges. He became less resentful.

These are deeply rooted issues. At a minimum, try to have compassion for each other's struggles with the kids.

How to Talk to Your Mate about Parenting Differences: Dos and Don'ts

DO:

- Bear in mind that your partner loves her child, even if she clashes with him.
- Recognize parent-child relationships are very hard to change.
- Know that even if you're right, criticizing her daughter will hurt her.
- *Empathize* with his distress, guilt, sorrow, or pride in his son even if you can't share the feelings.
- Speak calmly and constructively about your concerns. Explain how *you* have a stake because his behavior affects you directly or causes you worry about him.

Don't:

- Characterize your mate's parenting with demeaning names (wimp, doormat, tyrant) or call her child names (user, baby, taker).
- Expect change to happen quickly, if at all.
- Confront your partner's child directly; that's the parent's role.
- Badmouth your stepkids to others.

How to Handle Differences About Money for the Kids

If you two have built legal firewalls around your own assets, you'll never squabble about money you give your kids. Right? Nope.

Money is emotional. Maybe you grew up feeling you should be generous to yourself and the people you love. Or maybe your family taught you that, rich or poor, you should never spend a dime more than is necessary.

These differences can be irritating. One newly partnered couple in their seventies, both financially comfortable, quibbled over spending. She felt they should use their money (hers and his) to enjoy life. She describes him as "careful with the dollar." His mindset annoyed her, but never seriously. "I valued the relationship enough to stifle my irritation," she says. She made sure *she* didn't deny herself anything. Over time, she says, "I helped him be freer about money, and he's come along. We still laugh about his wanting to save on some tiny thing on our cruise. At the time, I turned to him and said, 'Are you *kidding* me?'"

These differences in values spill over to money you spend on your kids and grandkids. Even if it's your money, your kids, and your choice, don't be surprised if your mate second-guesses you.

Roger,* for example, frets about the large Christmas presents his wife (whom he adores) gives her kids and grandkids. He gets upset that she "helps" her adult sons with major expenses like starting a business, renovating a kitchen, or building a house. Once she gives one son or daughter so many thousands of dollars, she feels it's only fair to give the same to the others. She can afford it, Roger says, but he feels they don't appreciate her generosity. That bothers him. "They're not real good at saying thank you," he says.

She doesn't agree. "He came from a frugal family," she says. "Not poor, but they didn't spend money easily." She wants to *help* her kids achieve their goals, she says, and it gives her pleasure to do it. "It's a little frustrating to hear him ask whether the kids really deserve all that."

He knows the choice is hers. Still, he says he worries that she'll run out of funds if she someday has a long-term health condition. "I have long-term care insurance," he says. "She says she'll get it, but she hasn't yet."

For another couple in their seventies, it's the husband who helps his child and adult grandchild with thousands of dollars. His wife has given up talking to him about it. She worries he'll someday run out of money and she'll have to support him, but she doesn't think that's likely. She's more distressed at what she sees as an unhealthy dynamic between her husband and his child.

If you're the one criticizing how he's using his money, and his spending doesn't affect you, stay out of it. It's part of his lifelong history with them. It can mean anything from love and generosity to guilt for parenting offenses to emotional bribery for current attentions. Whether it's healthy or unhealthy, it's unlikely to change. Also be aware that what sounds like ingratitude or disrespect to you may feel different to your partner. The one *inside* the relationship hears things differently from the one *outside*.

If you're the big spender (or tightwad) fielding criticism, stay open to your partner's perspective. She may see something you can't. If you dislike hearing her comments, tell her you don't find them helpful and you'd like her to stop. Ultimately, how you spend your money is your choice.

Strengthen Your Couple Bond: Support Your Partner's Struggle with a Troubled Child

Some shy away from a potential mate who has a troubled child. If you've chosen to go forward, you've probably decided you have the emotional bandwidth to meet the challenge. If the child's trouble arises after you've committed to your relationship, support your partner however you can.

Some people cope by choosing a LAT relationship. Even so, if you're the one feeling devastated by your child's trauma, you'll look to your partner for emotional support. Eleanor* found this support with Miles.* When they met, she was in her late sixties, he was in his early seventies, and her son, Jason,* was in his early twenties. Jason* was an addict, living on the streets, occasionally becoming violent. When Miles heard about Eleanor's heartbreaking situation, he was filled with admiration. "She is one of the strongest women I've ever met," he says. "She struggles with some horrific stuff, but he's her son, and until you're in her shoes, you can't tell what that's like. And yet she stays positive about life."

They both felt it best to live apart so that Jason could feel he had a home to return to when he was ready. Eleanor sees Miles as a very special man. He not only sympathizes with her plight, he doesn't second-guess how she handles it. That's crucial to *their* relationship.

You have to tell yourself, and believe, says therapist Lois Nightingale, "'I'm not going to try to change them or shame them. I'm not going to tell them they're enmeshed with their addict child and enabling that child."

How to Support Your Partner's Parenting a Troubled Child

- Empathize. Even if *you* think his child's troubles are self-inflicted (excessive spending, for example, or chronic unemployment), recognize that the person you love is suffering.
- If she turns to you for help, listen, be supportive, and make suggestions carefully.
- If you have relevant experience—with, for example, addiction, depression, or incarceration—share what you know. If her child is open to it (and your partner agrees), share your experience with your stepchild.
- Do not join the chorus of friends and relatives telling his beleaguered mother what she should do: cut him off, let him live in the streets, stop babying him, tell him it's rehab or else.
- If the child's situation and your partner's distress get worse, encourage them to seek professional help. Participate if appropriate.

Cherish the Joys of Your New Family Connections

In this chapter, I've focused on the *problems* posed by your children. If you've approached each other's families with sensitivity and patience, you may be feeling lucky to have these new family members in your life.

I encourage you, if you haven't already done so, to take advantage of your partner's strengths. A positive outgoing person who is new to a family can, over time, bring fresh perspective and new enthusiasm to family relationships.

New York City psychoanalyst Sue Kolod told me of two fathers who had been distant from their daughters during their childhood and after. One was a workaholic who'd spent little time with his family. Another had been a womanizer. In each case, she says, the father's new wife reached out and formed a relationship with her husband's daughter. The wife helped her husband and his daughter reconnect and repair their relationship.

"We all long for community and emotional connection," Kolod says. "When someone new comes into the family system, it's a breath of fresh air. It opens things up. If the relationship is a good one with good feelings, we can have young and old people in our lives. It can help us see things a little differently."

Grandchildren, for example, can offer childless people rich experiences previously unknown to them. Young grandkids rarely make the distinction between a grandma and a step-grandma. If you act the role, you get the love.

Josie, sixty, childless herself, has developed close relationships with her partner's children. "I have grandkids now!" she says. "That's something I never thought I'd have in my life."

Jeff,* in his seventies and remarried about a decade, has a "unique bond" with his wife's grandkids, ages two to fourteen. "With the young ones," he says, speaking of the two- and four-year-old, "we play Touch the Sky, where I lift them to the ceiling and let them reach it." With the kids between eight and ten, he plays "Monster." He ignores them at first when they tap his back and run away. Then when they twist an imaginary key on his back, he says, "I turn into a monster and chase them with arms outstretched, running hunched over and grunting."

As he enumerates the various games he's made up, it's clear to me that this man likes to *play*. The satisfaction he gets from these little ones is immense, but there's more. With an older grandson, a cross-country runner—as Jeff was in high school—he's become a mentor and gets to pass down a part of himself to the next generation.

"The grandkids have brought a lot into my life," he says. "They've also helped to strengthen what was already a strong bond between my wife and me. At first it was just us, because I didn't know the grandkids, and some weren't even born yet. Now we *share* things about the grandkids."

This immersion in a partner's family life is not for everyone. You and your partner will make your own decisions and be guided by what you want and what's possible.

Chapter Eleven

Meet the Challenges, and Savor Every Moment

When you partner later in life, you know viscerally that your time together is limited. Gratitude, extra thoughtfulness, and a forgiving attitude toward flaws sweeten your intimacy.

Scholars Torbjörn Bildtgård and Peter Öberg, who study older couples, speak of a paradox: The shortness of time left, which frightens some people, also intensifies and enriches relationships. On the other hand, the wealth of available free time in the present fosters greater emotional intimacy than ever before. Most of those studied see their later-life union as their "crowning" relationship.

You can't stop the progress of time or wall off the effects of age, even with daily workouts at the gym. But you *can* help each other be as healthy as possible. When health problems come your way, you can meet them as a team.

The ways you've learned to talk to and trust each other will help you through life's toughest trials. When illness or disability threatens to divide you, compassion and honesty can bring you together.

Start now by taking a few practical measures to ease what may come.

Think *Hard* about Who You Want to Make Decisions for You If You Can't

Put it in writing and discuss with everyone—now!

While researching my previous book, *They're Your Parents, Too!: How Siblings Can Survive Their Parents' Aging Without Driving Each Other Crazy*, I heard some pretty awful stories of tearful, screaming adult children protesting a sibling's decision. "Don't put her in a home! Don't pull the plug! I know what she wants; you don't." Unfortunately, conflicts like these could erupt between your partner and your kids.

Here's what you can do to minimize such conflict.

Think through who in your life is likeliest to carry out your wishes if you're unable to make decisions yourself. Then discuss with your partner whom you want to appoint as health care proxy (also called power of attorney or POA) and why. Whether you're married, cohabiting, or in a LAT union may or may not affect this choice. Couples I talked to about this made different choices. In some cases, a wife appointed her son proxy, while her husband appointed her. Think about all the possible scenarios and circumstances. Then do what's best for *you*.

Be sure you discuss your reasons with family members. Also, most important, tell them clearly *what* you want to happen if you can't decide for yourself. If you'd like to be cared for at home as long as possible and that's feasible, say so. If you want to fight for every day of life versus end your pain quickly, be clear. Recognize that acting according to your wishes may be hard emotionally. Even if your mate and your kids get along splendidly, you *must* record your wishes legally in the form of a health care proxy (power of attorney, or POA) and a living will. You'll also have to select a proxy to handle your finances—which, in turn, allows your POA for health to pay for the kind of care you want. Sometimes that's the same person. Sometimes it's not. If it's not, they need to be able to cooperate for your benefit.

Bear in mind, says counselor Allison Forti, that your kids can present an obstacle to having your wishes carried out. They tend to be more protective of their parent and less pragmatic. It's easier for two older people to consider hard choices. "Kids in their thirties and forties may be less developmentally able to wrap their heads around these issues," she says.

Whether you choose your mate, a child or someone else as your health care proxy and financial proxy, make sure you sign a HIPPA Medical Release so your doctors can talk to whomever you wish about your health.

Do all these things *now.* Think the issues through. Discuss them with your loved ones. Create legal documents to ensure that things happen the way you want. Then put them all away and just savor every day. (And every six months or annually, confirm that your plans haven't changed.)

Encourage Good Health Habits in Each Other

You'd think that at our age, we'd all be working hard to keep ourselves healthy. Nah. Some of us mean well but get lazy or just aren't in the mood. We don't keep our resolutions to lose weight. If we're lucky, we've picked a partner with either a similar or a complementary level of health behavior, whether that's careful attention to diet, exercise, and doctors' visits or a more laid-back approach: What will be will be.

Now, I'm hardly perfect about this. I try to pay attention to diet and exercise. But I have lapses and then struggle to get back to my healthier routines. I am, however, always concerned about the health of my partner, Michael. Having been widowed (twice!), *I* think I'm justified. Be that as it may, my attempts with him range from mildly helpful to abysmally not.

Before I committed to a relationship with Chris, who was obese, I asked whether he'd lose weight. He vowed to do so, and he worked at it. He was never thin, but we were avid cyclists, and he was generally healthy. We couldn't have predicted the cancer that would kill him.

With Michael, my partner of five years, I worry about his sedentary lifestyle. Early on, I talked seriously to him about how Alan's denial of his heart condition had killed him. Michael listened. He took it in. He agreed to attend more to his health. He agreed to switch with me to a brilliant older doctor referred by people we trusted. Michael had some health issues, nothing terrible, and he was scrupulous about taking his medications.

Exercising more was one of our doctor's recommendations. Michael doesn't exercise enough (according to me). So I "remind" him. He gets annoyed. Trust me: not a health benefit.

At our last physical, when we were in the doctor's consulting room before our exams, Michael told the doctor he was feeling fine. He and I had agreed that when we went to the doctor together, it was okay to ask questions and make comments on the other's behalf. So I listed five or so observations about Michael's recent health or behavior that concerned me. After our separate physical exams, our doctor came out to the waiting room and spoke to me. "He's fine," he said.

"He's got a number of things wrong that won't kill him and that we're not going to do anything about." Then he looked at me with a twinkle in his eye. "Listen," he said, "I've been around the block a few times. Let *him* call the shots."

Well, I'd been told. Now, most of the time I think before I speak, and I often shut my mouth.

Jean, who is seventy-eight to her partner's eighty-one, has also begun to refrain from giving him health advice. "He can be very stubborn, especially about his health," she says. "It bothers me, but I'm learning that I need to back off and let him handle it."

Lowell, eighty-four, gives his partner, Barbara, eighty-one, credit for his developing better health habits. "She's more concerned with taking care of herself, and it rubbed off on me," he says. "I wasn't the most healthy eater, and we'd have conversations about food. She'd say, 'Oh, this is much better to eat.' Then we'd talk about the reasons why. I eat more vegetables now, less meat, and more fish, and we try to stay away from fried food. A hamburger is a special treat."

They exercise together: go to the gym three times a week, walk every day, do water aerobics. He's motivated partly, he says, by living in a senior community where he sees a lot of people deteriorating. "We don't want that to happen to us."

If *you* feel your partner is not attending to her health, here's what you *can* do: Sit down together, express your worry along with your love and your wish to be together as long as possible. Don't criticize or characterize what he is doing.

You get to do this once, says therapist Heather Williams. "Then *drop* it," she says. "If you become too wrapped up in the other person's problems, you get into a pursuer/distancer dynamic." If the pursuer stops pursuing something, she explains, changing their partner's health habits, for example, then that person may feel freer to do it.

Be a Team for Good Health

Married couples are healthier than single people, at least when they're in a good relationship. Study after study has shown this effect. It's almost certainly true that committed cohabitating couples share this benefit and probably also LAT couples.

Why does being half of a couple work this way? Apart from love and companionship—no small things!—each one models good health for the other. They remind each other: "It's time for our annual physicals"; "Don't forget to refill that prescription." If you fall down, or have a seizure or a heart attack, your partner's likely to be on hand: "Call 911!"

You may be able to encourage healthier habits in each other. But be aware that your power is limited. Habits are lifelong and not easy to change. Coaxing sweetly and lovingly sometimes helps. Nagging? I wish.

These are some constructive steps:

- Be a good example. If you join a walkers' club, she may go along.
- Do healthy things that are *fun*! Urging something because it's *good for you*? Deadly. What's fun for you? Cycling? Hiking? Dancing?
- Apply this principle for diet (but never call it that!). Take turns choosing restaurants. Or cooking. When it's your turn, make delicious and healthy food. If one dish becomes a favorite, you've achieved a small victory.
- Select good doctors and go to appointments together. You're likelier to give your doctors complete and accurate information.

Together, you're also better able to hear what your doctors say, then clarify with questions. As one seventy-eight-year-old husband told me, "It's always better to have another set of ears so we don't miss anything. Or I can pipe up and tell the doctor what she forgot to say."

Seeing doctors together also reduces distortions due to anxiety. One woman in her early seventies accompanied her partner on his first visit to a pulmonologist. In the consulting room after his breathing tests, the doctor explained that he had mild COPD (chronic obstructive pulmonary disease). At "COPD," he froze.

"Is the condition progressive?" asked his partner, to find out whether this form of COPD gets worse over time. "The doc said no," she later told me, "but he looked like a deer in the headlights. I turned to him and said, 'Sweetheart, this is great news. Your breathing is almost normal, and there's no reason it should get worse.' Then the doctor reassured him."

Along with established health habits, each of you has different experiences of illness and interacting with the medical system. You develop trustful or distrusting attitudes, for example. "Expecting them to change will only lead to disappointment," says University of Rochester Medical Center therapist Carol Ann Podgorski.

Sometimes a major health scare jolts people enough to clean up their act. You don't wish for that, of course, but do know that it can happen.

Embrace Your Differences

You hear women complain that their husband doesn't go to the doctor. It's true that men attend less to their health than women do, but not always, says Susan McDaniel, a family therapist at the University of Rochester Medical Center.

Suzanne Miller, a health behavior expert at Fox Chase Cancer Center in Philadelphia, has identified two basic personality types categorized by how they cope with anxiety about their health. People she calls "monitors" seek out as much information as they can, notice symptoms, see their doctors as soon as possible, and seek reassurance. Monitors exist on a spectrum. At one end are those who are rational and constructive and make well-informed decisions. At the other extreme are people who devour everything on the Internet, however crazy, overreact to the smallest sniffle, and obsessively go to doctors. All this makes them more anxious.

The other group, "blunters," avoid anxiety-laden issues. They don't read up on symptoms and are slow to seek medical help. At the most extreme end are people who deny real health concerns.

Those in the moderate middle, says McDaniel, exemplify different approaches. Neither is pathological, and you can help each other. "Blunters can help monitors from going off the deep end," she says, "and monitors can get blunters to the doctor and go along to make sure they say what's supposed to be said. Sometimes they polarize and fight about their differences and whether a partner's health situation is serious. But if they can accept their differences and compromise, each style has something to offer."

Blunters tend to think through health issues rationally, monitors more emotionally. "If he can speak to her anxiety, and she can appeal to his rational side, their communication should go better," she says.

One late-seventies couple uses their different styles to advantage.

He stays calm and doesn't look for information. With any symptom, she gets frantically anxious and imagines the worst. He looks at each situation calmly and doesn't get ahead of himself.

As a monitor, she wants to know everything. She's been wearing a wrist device that registers her heart rate on her smartphone. This turned out to be a very good thing: She noticed that her heart rate never varied—not normal! "I felt scared," she says. They went right to their doctor; she needed a pacemaker.

The day of the operation, he was calm; she was terrified she'd never wake from the anesthesia. "I didn't want to die," she says. "He kept me as calm as I could possibly be. He'd pat my shoulder and kiss me. He'd reassure me: 'Everything will be fine.'"

He was convincing, I believe, because that was his outlook: *Everything will be fine.*

Whichever personality type you are, you may want to tread carefully around your partner's anxiety about a disease that killed the late spouse. When Chris and I were married, for example, I was especially alert to signals of the heart disease that killed Alan. Chris was especially sensitive to the breast cancer from which his wife died.

Myra,* who married a widower as she was turning seventy, recently went for a mammogram without telling her husband. His wife died of breast cancer, she explains. "I only told him after I got my good report," she says. Had there been a problem, she would have had to tell him. "Why cause him anxiety waiting for results?" she says.

This was my approach with Chris, and I think it makes sense. It would be better, however, says Allison Forti, if partners agree up front how they'll handle health updates and tests. If you don't agree first, she says, "you limit your intimacy, and the one having the test has to go through her anxiety alone. I lean more toward genuineness and transparency, as long as you are on the same page about it."

If She Has a Disability, Learn What It Means to Her;
If You're the One, Learn How It Affects Your Partner

If you develop a disability, it may seem a minor inconvenience to your partner. (Did you ever hear this one: What's the difference between major surgery and minor surgery? Major surgery is when it's happening to *you*.)

On the other hand, you may overreact and treat him like an invalid. Not good. Micromanaging or infantilizing him damages your relationship. Listen harder to what he's telling you he *can* do.

Howard and Elaine, now nearing eighty, have generally adjusted well to his loss of vision due to glaucoma. He's now legally blind, seeing the world as if through an opaque plastic bag, everything hazy. No question this condition has been challenging, for both of them.

With a rehab teacher, Howard learned to manage the white cane he uses to walk down the street. On his own, he's improved. "I got a longer cane," he says, "so I can walk at my own pace. I'm six-three and have a longer stride."

Their accommodation to this change didn't happen automatically. At first she waited on him and smothered him. Not necessary for him; not good for them. So they consulted a marital and family counselor.

"I wanted my wife to understand what it's like to live with a partially sighted person," Howard says. "She has to understand I'm gonna step on her tiny feet. I do that in the kitchen, and she yells, 'Ouch!'" ("And we're not dancing!" she interjects playfully.)

It was hard, but Elaine needed to give him his freedom. "If he was going to screw up, he'd screw up. Apart from driving, he's allowed to do everything, including use a sharp knife. If he cuts himself, he cuts himself," she says, accepting though clearly not happy about it.

She's gotten better, according to Howard. Still, he says, "I feel like I could do more than I do, but she does it first." With a teasing laugh, he adds, "Maybe it's just her natural bossiness."

Some newly disabled people feel their partner isn't paying *enough* attention to the change. If you now have to wear an oxygen tank when you go out, she may ask, "What's the big deal?" But if all your life you've been a natty dresser, shoes polished to a mirror shine and hat perched at a rakish angle, that old guy with the oxygen just isn't you. You find it humiliating.

To come together, you need to talk more intimately than maybe ever before. Even the closest couples can stumble. In one case, a husband in his eighties resisted using his walker and refused outright to sit in a wheelchair. His wife felt lonely and isolated. She missed their dinners with friends, going to museums and theater. But these activities required walking distances that her husband couldn't manage. If only he'd use a wheelchair, they could still do the things they loved. What was the big deal?

"I'm not going to be one of those drooling idiots in a wheelchair," he responded. End of conversation.

At a miserable stalemate, they consulted therapist Kathryn Chefetz, of the older adults psychotherapy project at the Washington School of Psychiatry. Chefetz helped the husband express the fears behind his resistance. The biggest was that his friends would see him as a lesser person. His wife expressed her fear that she was losing him.

"His coming to terms with the situation was quite a process, and his wife was often frustrated," Chefetz says. Over time, he recognized that most of his fears were not grounded in reality. By the time his birthday rolled around, he was ready to embrace the present from his wife: a motorized scooter. He loved riding it and the freedom it opened up for him.

The refusal to use such health devices is common. "It's very public," says therapist Allison Forti. "You want to be as 'normal' as possible. Build compassion for yourself, your partner, and for the situation.

That can lessen resentment and lead to better communication. It helps each person have appreciation and respect for what the other is going through. This is *hard*, but couples can become closer."

If You Have a Disability, Hold Up Reality to Your Fears; If Your Partner's the One, Apply Compassion

If You Have a New Disability . . .

A sense of loss often accompanies new limits. You *have* lost some precious ability, so let yourself grieve. But don't hide out because of your fears.

To overcome them, write them down:

- People won't see me as the same person.
- Our friends won't want to hang out with us anymore.
- People will get annoyed that I need to go slow.
- My partner will leave me.

Now check out your fears against the reality. Ask your partner how *she* feels. Talk to your friends and family. One healthy eighty-four-year-old man told me that at their senior community, he and his partner socialize with lots of people who use walkers and other assistive devices. "No one looks down on them," he says.

Be aware that people take their cues from you. If you behave like the same person on the inside, they're likelier to treat you that way. Also think of people you know who have disabilities. Are people shunning them? Do they sit in a corner, or are they still the life of the party? Maybe they're somewhere in between.

"If your friends think you have a glass-half-full approach, they're likelier to come 'round," says medical therapist Podgorski, who holds degrees in public health as well as marriage and family therapy.

To develop a more positive attitude, make another list. Write down all the things you can still do, especially if you don't hide out. Include both physical and mental strengths and activities you can still enjoy. For example, if you use a walker, you might list:

- I can still get around, just more slowly.
- I can enjoy food and wine just as much.
- My hearing isn't bad.
- My mind is still sharp.
- My sight is good.

Explain to your love how this change feels to *you*. Then ask how it's affecting *her*.

If Your Partner Is Newly Coping with a Disability . . .

Learn what it's like for her and what it *means* to her. If she needs but refuses to use an oxygen tank, for example, lovingly probe why. Make her feel safe to express her fears or grief. Reassure her.

- Explain how this change (or how he's coping with it) affects you. Are you feeling more isolated? Are you worried that without his walker, he'll hurt himself?
- Brainstorm ways to make this change easier. If, say, a few people do react negatively, choose to spend more time with others who don't.

Illness Challenges You but Can Knit
You Together More Tightly

Nobody welcomes illness. The pain and fear can make you each feel more alone. But you also have a chance to grow intimate in a more profound way if you share your deepest feelings.

Often a health crisis sharpens your love with the specter of loss. Dorothy, eighty, experienced this with her husband's cardiac emergency: surgery to repair his aortic valve. "I was afraid I might lose him," she says, "and I badly want more years with him. For me, the word 'cherish' resonates even more than 'love.'"

Maxi* and Suzanne* are a recently married couple in their fifties. When Maxi developed a mysterious autoimmune disorder, the stress and fear were intense and different for each.

"I found this person I love and want to be with," Suzanne says. "She may never get better and may get worse." Even while terrified of losing Maxi, she says, "Her illness felt annoying and hard. Hard responsibilities fell on my shoulders, like having to do all the shopping and other chores."

For Maxi, her partner's steadfast presence meant everything. "Knowing someone will stay feels healing," she says.

Just as Maxi was feeling better, Suzanne had to be hospitalized. The exhaustion of her wife's illness had led to an "adrenal crisis," she says, "and I was sick for several months." After her release, she was mostly bedridden. "My wife had to help me up and down the stairs for weeks."

The crisis brought their relationship to a deeper level. "I know she has my back and vice versa," Suzanne says. "I'm really confident that she will come through. We like each other as well as love each other, and after each crisis, we find our way back to each other." The crisis taught her more: "All my life, I had a huge fear that I'd always have to be in charge and be the responsible one, and I broke through it with her. Now I know I can depend on her and be vulnerable and open and weak and still be loved."

During her long periods of taking care of Maxi, Suzanne sometimes felt angry. That's common for caregivers. If you react this way, don't feel guilty. Instead, find a way to take a time-out. Figure out what you need most—maybe just ordinary companionship with a healthy friend or daily long walks. Make it happen.

Confronting a dire diagnosis can make both the positive and negative effects on the relationship more intense. Forti, who works with cancer patients, has seen this happen. With cancer, she explains, you're forced to let your partner *see* you, no pretense. There's no attention to prettying up and being on your best behavior. After chemo, suffering nausea and baldness, you'll hide nothing, so you lose your fear of showing yourself.

"This is more so for the person going through treatment," Forti says, "but that's contagious, and partners become equally vulnerable and authentic."

She recalls a couple in their fifties. The woman's cancer was diagnosed early, but the five-year survival rate was low. The man and woman recognized that for their relationship to work, they'd have to take care of their own needs as well as respect each other's. The patient's boyfriend thought he could handle the situation as long as they kept to a LAT arrangement. In a compromise, he rented an apartment next door. This allowed them to see each other easily and spend several nights a week together. But they marked out clear boundaries. She could say when she wasn't feeling up to seeing him, and he could say when he needed time alone.

Forti describes her as a spunky woman who's never once

complained about her partner. "She lights up when she talks about him," Forti says.

For his part, he loves how funny his lover is; he's fond of her quirks. After a long, unhappy marriage, he's found a woman with whom he can laugh—despite her illness or sometimes at it. And like many people in his situation, he's discovered capacities in himself that he never suspected and sees himself in a new light. He feels good that he enjoys taking care of another person. He thinks of himself as more giving than he'd realized. He likes himself better.

They were lucky. She beat the odds and is doing well after ten years. But their rewards began early. "They have a rich appreciation and trust and respect for each other," Forti says. "These are the building blocks of a healthy relationship. If you've got this, there's something magical."

No one wishes for cancer to deepen their relationship. Still, it's worth noting how dropping our pretenses and daring to be nakedly who we are can powerfully enhance our intimacy.

Live in the Moment: Treasure Your Time Together

Sometimes we toss off grandiose wishes about our longevity; we fend off anxiety with humor. Chris used to say he wanted to die at 103, having sex while skydiving. I'd tell him I was fine dying at 103 in the act, but no way I was jumping out of a plane.

We have no idea whether we'll live another thirty years or make it through the next day. Whatever your health condition, you feel lucky to have each other. If you keep growing in the ways that have brought you to this fortunate place, you'll find joy all your lives, even as age chips away at your body.

As one sixty-six-year-old woman expresses it: "This is so good we don't dare not grab it. There's not a ton of time left. We've had five years so far, and we'd like it to be twenty-five. That's not likely. But what time we do have will be really sweet."

Cultivate These Habits to Age Beautifully as a *Couple*

Many of the couples I've introduced you to have deeply moved me. Whether they've been together three years, ten, or even a lucky twenty, they feel grateful for their unique love. They prize it even more, knowing their time together is short. Illness and disability challenge them, for sure, but they savor every day.

These couples share some positive attitudes and habits. These can also help *you* through the tough times:

- Communicate as honestly and intimately as you can, sharing your fears, reaffirming your love, asking for what you need and asking what your partner needs.
- Spend more time with people you enjoy. One wife told me that she and her spouse spend less time with family who stress them, but more with others of all ages. "We welcome happiness in our lives. And having little kids around is very life-affirming," she says.
- Build a new network of friends or people who can offer you comfort and solace when you need it.
- Practice gratitude. When illness grinds you down, cultivate gratitude more consciously: 1) Before a meal or at the end of the day, write down three things you're grateful for. 2) When you feel irritated with your partner, think of one thing about her that you love, like a bubbling laugh or an affectionate caress

> when you need it, and focus on that. 3) Seek out beauty in art
> or nature; this can make gratitude well up in you.
>
> - Reflect on the life you've had and see yourself spiritually or
>   philosophically within the natural cycle of life.
> - Most of all, as you spend the last months or years with the
>   person you dearly love, cherish every moment.

Young people find it strange that older folks are less scared of death than they are. Research confirms this. We don't worry about the future so much. We live in the moment more. "All we can be sure of is *now*," says Dorothy, "and it brings us closer together."

Jean, seventy-eight, says she doesn't worry about the end. "However much time the good Lord gives us, I'm enjoying it," she says.

Lowell, eighty-four, says that he and his partner, Barbara, eighty-one, don't think about mortality. "We stay busy enough that we don't have time for that," he says.

Elaine and Howard exemplify this attitude. Despite Howard's limited sight, they're exploring the country in their motor home, frequently pedaling their adult tricycles. Looking ahead, Elaine says, "If our health goes south, we'll come home and live in our house and hire people to come in and care for us. We'll be together as long as we possibly can, and we'll love each other until it's over.

"I go to sleep in his arms," she says, "and we wake up together. I'm so happy it hurts."

Acknowledgments

Iowe a debt of gratitude to the people who helped me create this book and get it out into the world. To start at the beginning, I'd like to thank my agent Jane von Mehren at Aevitas Creative Management, who, with patience and know-how, helped me turn a ten-page idea into a formidable proposal that would appeal to the likes of an editor like Priscilla Painton at Simon & Schuster.

I can't say enough about the amazing Priscilla. At our first solo meeting, she drilled into my soul and said, "Your biggest challenge as a journalist will be to speak in your own voice to write a self-help book." Over uncountable drafts of the first chapters, she dragged me (inwardly kicking and screaming) to write a book that I believe *will* help readers, a book of which I'm very proud. She also worked her magic to bring AARP into the mix and with it, AARP's excellent book editor Jodi Lipson, whose savvy eye helped polish the manuscript even further.

Priscilla's wonderful assistant, Hana Park, worked tirelessly and well on helping me achieve the right tone, and she was a wizard at organizing the mass of material. Both she and Priscilla offered enthusiastic support and encouragement throughout.

I am grateful to my friends and family who early on believed in my germ of an idea for a book and urged me forward. I am especially grateful to my dear friend and fellow writer Alice Feiring, who gave me boosts when I was feeling low and sometimes helped me out of a dilemma with her excellent writer's eye. I am also grateful to my dear friend Rick, who never lets me get away with shortcuts or half-truths.

I owe a debt to the many experts—psychological, sociological, medical, and legal—who gave me the benefit of their expertise and wisdom on every dimension of this complex subject of love after fifty.

Most of all I want to thank the many women and men who opened their souls to my probing questions, sometimes reliving painful memories. I felt privileged and deeply moved when they shared, often tearfully, the depth of their joy in their later-life loves.

Finally, I am grateful to my partner, Michael, for reaffirming that love only gets better with age.

Resources

Headwork

Therapy and Counseling

For individual therapists: www.findapsychologist.org.

For emotion-focused therapy (EFT): www.iceeft.com/find-a-therapist.

Support Groups

www.psychologytoday.com/us/therapists. Look at the last/bottom filter on the left, where a "Groups" specialty can be found (under the "See Nearest" category).

Books on Personal Growth

Gillihan, Seth J. *Cognitive Behavioral Therapy Made Simple: 10 Strategies for Managing Anxiety, Depression, Anger, Panic, and Worry.* Emeryville, CA: Althea Press, 2018.

Burns, David. *Feeling Great: The Revolutionary New Treatment for Depression and Anxiety.* Eau Claire, WI: PESI Publishing and Media, 2020.

Martin, Sharon, and Julie de Azevedo Hanks. *The CBT Workbook for Perfectionism: Evidence-Based Skills to Help You Let Go of Self-Criticism, Build Self-Esteem, and Find Balance.* Oakland, CA: New Harbinger, 2019.

Rubens, Richard. *Polarities of Experience: The Psychology of the Real.* New York: Popolano Press, 2017.

Williams, Mark, and Danny Penman. *Mindfulness: An Eight-Week Plan for Finding Peace in a Frantic World.* Emmaus, Pennsylvania: Rodale Books, 2012.

Williams, Mark, John Teasdale, Zindel Segal, and Jon Kabat-Zinn. *The Mindful Way Through Depression.* New York: The Guilford Press, 2007.

Tolle, Eckhart. *The Power of Now.* Novato, CA: New World Library, 2004.

Divorce Recovery

www.divorcecare.org.

Covy, Karen. "The Ultimate List of Divorce Support Groups and Why You Need One." www.karencovy.com/divorce-support-groups-can-make-divorce-easier/.

Beattie, Melody. *Codependent No More: How to Stop Controlling Others and Start Caring for Yourself.* Center City, MN: Hazelden, 1986.

Trafford, Abigail. *Crazy Time: Surviving Divorce and Building a New Life,* Third Edition. New York: William Morrow Paperbacks, 2014.

Help for the Widowed

Tetrault, Sam. "8 Best Support Groups for People Who Lost a Spouse or Partner." www.joincake.com/blog/widow-support-groups/.

- "Online Support Groups for Someone Who Lost a Partner"
- "Tips for Finding an In-Person Support Group."

To Reduce Loneliness

- Meetup.com: You can meet with people who share your interests: anything from dining to making flies for fly fishing to Elizabethan history to knitting to gardening to golfing. If you can't find a group you want, you can start one of your own.
- Take a college course.
- Sixtyandme.com: networking groups for women over sixty.
- Join (or start) a book club.
- Senior centers (search locally) and aging-in-place social organizations.

Dating

Brown, Sandra L. *How to Spot a Dangerous Man Before You Get Involved.* Alameda, CA: Hunter House, 2005.

Feuerman, Marni. *Ghosted and Bread Crumbed: Stop Falling for Unavailable Men and Get Smart About Healthy Relationships.* Novato, CA: New World Library, 2019.

Jordan, Christie. *Online Dating for Women Over 40: The Hopeful Woman's 10 Step Guide to Enjoyment and Success.* Orinda, CA: BluePoint Press, 2013.

Manly, Carla Marie. *Aging Fully: A Woman's Guide to Optimal Health, Relation-ships, and Fulfillment for her 50s and Beyond.* New York: Familius, LLC, 2019.

Sex
Therapists and Books on Sex

American Association of Sexuality Educators, Counselors and Therapists: www
.aasect.org.

Society for Sex Therapy & Research: sstarnet.org.

Kleinplatz, Peggy J., and A. Dana Ménard. *Magnificent Sex: Lessons from Ex-traordinary Lovers.* London: Routledge Press, 2020.

McCarthy, Barry, and Emily J. McCarthy. *Contemporary Men's Health: Con-fronting Myths and Promoting Change.* London: Routledge Press, 2020.

McCarthy, Barry, and Michael Metz. *Men's Sexual Health.* London: Routledge Press, 2007.

McCarthy, Barry, and Emily J. McCarthy. *Finding Your Sexual Voice: Celebrat-ing Female Sexuality.* London: Routledge Press, 2018.

Metz, Michael, and Barry McCarthy. *Coping with Erectile Dysfunctions: How to Regain Confidence and Enjoy Great Sex.* Oakland, CA: New Harbinger Publications, 2004.

Legal and Financial Guidance

At different stages of your relationship, you will need to make sure your wishes or agreements about money, housing, and health issues are established legally in documents for each purpose. If you cohabit or marry, you (and your families) will benefit from having a prenuptial or cohabitation agreement, or more spe-cific documents drawn up by your lawyers.

Marital and Family Law

American Academy of Matrimonial Lawyers: https://aaml.org/page/findalawyer.

Hurme, Sally Balch. *Checklist for My Family: A Guide to My History, Finan-cial Plans and Final Wishes.* American Bar Association, 2015. https://www
.amazon.com/ABA-AARP-Checklist-Family-Financial/dp/1627229825.

Marshall, Jeff. "How to Find a Good Lawyer for Older Adult Issues." https://
marshallelder.blogspot.com/2014/07/how-to-find-good-lawyer-for-older
-adult.html.

National Elder Law Foundation: https://nelf.org/search/custom.asp?id=5427.

National Association of Estate Planner and Councils (NAEPC): http://www
.naepc.org/designations/estate_planners/search#spec/All.

Adult Children and Family Dynamics

American Association of Marriage and Family Therapy (AAMFT): https://www
.aamft.org/therapistlocator.net.
Papernow, Patricia. *Surviving and Thriving in Stepfamily Relationships.* London:
Routledge Press, 2013.
Prosch, Tim. *The Other Talk: A Guide to Talking with Your Adult Children About
the Rest of Your Life.* New York: McGraw-Hill Education, 2013.

Health
Therapists for Older Adults and Medical Family Therapy

Some therapists have expertise with aging and health and will list this specialty
on their profile, which you will find at most of the therapy websites listed above.

A few mental health organizations specialize in therapy for older people. In
New York City, the Service Program for Older People (SPOP) offers low-cost
therapy for people over fifty-five. In Washington, D.C., Washington School of
Psychiatry offers therapy for older adults in their Center for the Aging.

If you'd like a counselor with expertise in certain diseases or with geriatric
issues, ask for referrals at your local medical center. Some hospitals and medical
care facilities have counselors on staff.

For End-of-Life Planning

Miller, B.J., and Shoshanna Berger. *A Beginner's Guide to the End: Everything
You Need to Know to Live Fully and Die Well.* New York: Simon & Schuster,
2019.
Russo, Francine. *They're Your Parents, Too!: How Siblings Can Survive Their Par-
ents' Aging Without Driving Each Other Crazy.* New York: Bantam Books,
2010.
Levine, Carol. *Navigating Your Later Years for Dummies.* Hoboken, NJ: For
Dummies, 2018.

Notes

Preface

ix The first one that I wrote about became a classic: Francine Russo, "Live-in Divorce: Tortured Couples Who Have to Live Together," *New York* magazine, Feb. 5, 1990.

ix My observation and research became: Francine Russo, *They're Your Parents, Too!: How Siblings Can Survive Their Parents' Aging Without Driving Each Other Crazy* (New York: Bantam Books, 2010).

x They showed how our longer life spans: Susan L. Brown and Matthew R. Wright, "Marriage, Cohabitation, and Divorce in Later Life," *Innovation in Aging* 1, no. 2 (September 2017); Susan L. Brown et al., "Later-Life Marital Dissolution and Repartnership Status: A National Portrait," *The Journals of Gerontology: Series B* 73, no. 6 (September 2018): 1032–1042.

xi Whether they meet online or another way: Gretchen Livingston, "Chapter 2: The Demographics of Remarriage," in *Four-in-Ten Couples Are Saying 'I Do,' Again* (Washington, D.C.: Pew Research Center, 2014), 10–15.

xi Add in couples who cohabitate: Brown, "Later-Life Marital Dissolution," 1032–1042; Brown, "Marriage, Cohabitation, and Divorce," 2017.

xi It's happening because we are the first to live: Susan L. Brown and I. Fen Lin, "The Gray Divorce Revolution: Rising Divorce Among Middle-Aged and Older Adults, 1990–2010," *The Journals of Gerontology: Series B* 67, no. 6 (2012): 731–41.

xi Research shows that as a group: Chaya Koren and S. Lipman-Schiby, "Not a Replacement: Emotional Experiences and Practical

Consequences of Israeli Second Couplehood Stepfamilies Constructed in Old Age," *Journal of Aging Studies*, no. 31 (2014): 70–82; Torbjörn Bildtgård and Peter Öberg, "Time As a Structuring Condition Behind New Intimate Relationships in Later Life," *Aging and Society* 35, no. 7 (2015): 1505–1528.

xi   As partners, you're probably more emotionally stable: Laura L. Carstensen, "The Influence of a Sense of Time on Human Development," *Science* 312, no. 5782 (2006); Laura L. Carstensen et al., "Emotional Experience Improves with Age: Evidence Based on Over 10 Years of Experience Sampling," *Psychology and Aging* 26, no. 1 (2011): 21–33; M. N. Shiota and R. W. Levenson, "Effects of Aging on Experimentally Instructed Detached Reappraisal, Positive Reappraisal, and Emotional Behavior Suppression," *Psychology and Aging* 24, no. 4 (2009): 890–900.

xi   In her study of couples in later-life second marriages: Koren, "Not a Replacement," 70–82.

xii Other researchers have found that later-life relationships offered more opportunities for psychological growth: Koren, "Not a Replacement," 70–82; Bildtgård, "Time As a Structuring Condition," 1505–1528.

xii This greater selfhood, psychologists: David Snarch, *Passionate Marriage: Keeping Love and Intimacy Alive in Committed Relationships* (New York: W. W. Norton, 2009); Donald Williamson, *The Intimacy Paradox: Personal Authority in the Family System* (New York: Guilford, 2002).

Chapter One

Do the Headwork

3   In study after study, Stanford's Laura: Laura L. Carstensen et al., "Emotional Experience Improves with Age: Evidence Based on Over 10 Years of Experience Sampling," *Psychology and Aging* 26, no. 1 (2011): 21–33.

4   If you're working, you're: Ruth Kanfer and Phillip L. Ackerman, "Aging, Adult Development, and Work Motivation," *Academy of Management Review* 29, no. 3 (2004).

11   When you do something for others: Robert A. Emmons and Michael E. McCullough, eds., *The Psychology of Gratitude* (New York, NY: Oxford University Press, 2004).

12   It can help you notice recurrent negative: Seth J. Gillihan, *Cognitive Behavioral Therapy Made Simple: 10 Strategies for Managing Anxiety, Depression, Anger, Panic, and Worry* (Emeryville, CA: Althea Press, 2018).

12   It can reduce depression, anger, and anxiety: Ibid.

12 Many disciplines use mindfulness: Ibid.
21 She was moved by a TED Talk by Amy Purdy: Amy Purdy, "Living Beyond Limits" TED Talk, TEDxOrangeCoast, May 2011, https://www.ted.com/talks/amy_purdy_living_beyond_limits ?language=en.
22 She shares many of these on her website: Patty Blue Hayes, https://www.pattybluehayes.com/.
23 I learned this practice in therapy: Gillihan, *Cognitive Behavioral Therapy*, 2018.

Chapter Two
Identify the Emotional Traits of Your Next Partner

46 You live more in the present: Laura L. Carstensen, "The Influence of a Sense of Time on Human Development," *Science* 312, no. 5782 (2006).

Chapter Four
Reconsider Your Automatic Categories

83 Studies show that most of us think of ourselves: David C. Rubin and Dorthe Berntsen, "People Over Forty Feel 20% Younger Than Their Age: Subjective Age Across the Lifespan," *Psychonomic Bulletin & Review* 13 (2006): 776–780.
83 Women pretend partly to combat the outmoded: Stephanie Coontz, *Marriage, a History: How Love Conquered Marriage* (New York: Penguin/Random House, 2006).

Chapter Five
Date as a Realist: Are Negative Attitudes or Fantasies Sabotaging You?

100 As author Seth J. Gillihan: Seth J. Gillihan, *Cognitive Behavioral Therapy Made Simple: 10 Strategies for Managing Anxiety, Depression, Anger, Panic, and Worry* (Emeryville, CA: Althea Press, 2018).

Chapter Six
Navigate the Emotional Currents of Dating

108 Set small, manageable goals: Seth J. Gillihan, *Cognitive Behavioral Therapy Made Simple: 10 Strategies for Managing Anxiety, Depression, Anger, Panic, and Worry* (Emeryville, CA: Althea Press, 2018).

Chapter Seven
Try a Relationship

124   Saying no to STD testing: Carla Marie Manly, *Aging Joyfully: A Woman's Guide to Optimal Health, Relationships, and Fulfillment for her 50s and Beyond* (New York: Familius, 2019).

133   But if you're drawn again and again: Richard Rubens, *Polarities of Experience: The Psychology of the Real* (New York: Popolano Press, 2017), 292–93.

Chapter Eight
Rediscover Sex—with a New Partner at a New Time of Life

146   Sex is good for your health: Stacy Tessler Lindau and Natalia Gavrilova, "Sex, Health, and Years of Sexually Active Life Gained Due to Good Health: Evidence from Two U.S. Population–Based Cross-Sectional Surveys of Ageing," *British Medical Journal* 340 (2010).

146   Kissing, caressing, or sexy talk: Michael Castleman, *Kissing* (Hoboken, NJ: John Wiley & Sons, 2015).

148   During and after sex, love hormones: Ibid.

154   Howard is typical of men: Barry McCarthy and Emily J. McCarthy, *Finding Your Sexual Voice: Celebrating Female Sexuality* (London: Routledge Press, 2018).

154   A newer model, advocated: Peggy J. Kleinplatz and A. Dana Ménard, *Magnificent Sex: Lessons from Extraordinary Lovers* (London: Routledge Press, 2020).

155   Researchers are finding that millions of people: Linda Fisher et al., *Sex, Romance, and Relationships: AARP Survey of Midlife and Older Adults* (Washington, D.C.: AARP, 2010). Pepper Schwartz, Sarah Diefendorf, and Anne McGlynn-Wright, "Sexuality in Aging," in *APA Handbook of Sexuality and Psychology: Vol. 1. Person-Based Approaches*, eds. D. L. Tolman and L. M. Diamond (Washington, D.C.: American Psychological Association, 2014), 523–551.

156   In her research on older people in second marriages: Chaya Koren and S. Lipman-Schiby, "Not a Replacement: Emotional Experiences and Practical Consequences of Israeli Second Couplehood Stepfamilies Constructed in Old Age," *Journal of Aging Studies*, no. 31 (2014): 70–82.

163 Women, if you're having more trouble reaching orgasm: Wiley, Diana, and Walter M. Bortz II. "Sexuality and Aging—Usual and Successful," *The Journals of Gerontology: Series A* 51A, no. 3 (1996): M142–M146.

165 Some men experience unpleasant side effects: Cunha, John P., ed., "Cialis (tadalafil) vs. Viagra (sildenafil)," MedicineNet, https://www.medicinenet .com/cialis_vs_viagra/article.htm.

165 Some people prefer Cialis: Ibid.

169 Even if you have trouble coming, you may experience: Pepper Schwartz and Nicholas Velotta, "Gender and Sexuality in Aging," in *Handbook of the Sociology of Gender*, 2nd ed., eds. Barbara J. Risman, Carissa M. Froyum, and William J. Scarborough (New York: Springer, 2018), 329–347.

170 If you're turned off by the term: Jayne Leonard, "Do ED Rings Work? What to Know, Plus Top Options," *Medical News Today*, June 30, 2020.

174 You can find a guide to these "sensate exercises" at Cornell Health: https:// health.cornell.edu/sites/health/files/pdf-library/sensate-focus.pdf.

174 In research to discover how to have: Kleinplatz, 2020.

Chapter Nine

Live Together or Not, Marry or Not: Create the Relationship You Need

177 Older couples like us are "at the forefront of family change": Susan L. Brown and Matthew R. Wright, "Marriage, Cohabitation, and Divorce in Later Life," *Innovation in Aging* 1, no. 2 (September 2017).

177 This wealth of choices, says: Jacquelyn J. Benson and Marilyn Coleman, "Older Adults Developing a Preference for Living Apart Together," *Journal of Marriage and Family* 78, no. 3 (2016): 797–812.

178 It goes along with major shifts in the U.S. and Europe: Benson, 2016.

186 Living apart increases your odds: Jenny DeJong Gierveld, "Intra-couple Caregiving of Older Adults Living Apart Together: Commitment and Independence," *Canadian Journal on Aging* 34, no. 3 (2015): 356–365.

186 This is one reason older couples increasingly: Gierveld, 2015.

186 Research shows, however, that despite expressing a wish *not* to take this role: Ibid.

188 Most older cohabitators are committed forever: Alisa C. Lewin, "Health and Relationship Quality Later in Life: A Comparison of Living Apart Together (LAT), First Marriages, Remarriages and Cohabitation," *Journal of Family Issues* 38, no. 12 (2017): 1754–1774.

Chapter Ten
Deal with the Kids—or Work Around Them

203 Carolyn's husband Jerry: Jerry Parr and Carolyn Parr, *In the Secret Service: The True Story of the Man Who Saved President Reagan's Life* (Chicago: Tyndale House Publishers, 2013).

204 It's a myth that *"The dog is dead and the kids are grown"*: Patricia Papernow, "The Remarriage Triangle: Working with Later-Life Recouplers and Their Grown Children," *Psychotherapy Networker* (January/February 2016): 49–53; Patricia Papernow, *Surviving and Thriving in Stepfamily Relationships* (London: Routledge Press, 2013).

Chapter Eleven
Meet the Challenges, and Savor Every Moment

225 Scholars Torbjörn Bildtgård and Peter Öberg, who study older couples: Torbjörn Bildtgård and Peter Öberg, "Time as a Structuring Condition Behind New Intimate Relationships in Later Life," *Aging and Society* 35, no. 7 (2015): 1505–1528.

226 While researching my previous book: Francine Russo, *They're Your Parents, Too!: How Siblings Can Survive Their Parents' Aging Without Driving Each Other Crazy* (New York: Bantam Books, 2010).

230 Married couples are healthier than single people: L. Waite and M. Gallagher, *The Case for Marriage: Why Married People Are Happier, Healthier and Better Off Financially* (New York: Doubleday, 2000).

232 It's true that men attend less to their health: Suzanne M. Miller, "Monitoring Versus Blunting Styles of Coping with Cancer Influence the Information Patients Want and Need About Their Disease: Implications for Cancer Screening and Management," *Cancer* 76: 2 (1995): 167–177.

About the Author

FRANCINE RUSSO is the author of *Love After 50: How to Find It, Enjoy It, and Keep It* and *They're Your Parents, Too!: How Siblings Can Survive Their Parents' Aging Without Driving Each Other Crazy*.

Armed with a PhD in English literature, she became a journalist, focusing on psychology, relationships, and social trends. Having cut her teeth at the *Village Voice*, she's gone on to write for virtually every major publication from the *Atlantic* to the *New York Times*. She contributed to the over-fifty beat at *Time* magazine for more than a decade, and her cover stories have appeared in publications from *Parade* and *Scientific American* to *New York* magazine. A dynamic and polished presenter, she is in great demand as a keynote speaker.

Francine has two grown children, three adult stepchildren, and six amazing grandkids (so far). She has experienced firsthand the tremendous potential we all have to grow and transform ourselves with the people we love. She lives in New York with her partner.